SAVE YOUR CHILD

*High Tech Children, Modern Life
and Spoiled Childhood*

N.K. SONDHI

GENERAL PRESS

Published by
GENERAL PRESS
4805/24, Fourth Floor, Krishna House
Ansari Road, Daryaganj, New Delhi - 110002
Ph : 011-23282971, 45795759
E-mail : generalpressindia@gmail.com

www.generalpress.in

© General Press

All rights reserved. No part of this publication may be reproduced, stored in a retrieval system, or transmitted, in any form or by any means—electronic, mechanical, photocopying, recording or otherwise—without the prior written permission of the publishers.

First Edition : 2018

ISBN : 9789388118361

1 7 1 2 2 0 1 8

Purchase our Books and eBooks online from:
Amazon.in | Flipkart.com | Play Store

Published by Azeem Ahmad Khan for General Press

Contents

N.K. Sondhi 7
Acknowledgement 9
Introduction 11

1. The Purpose of this Book. 13
2. Family Atmosphere. 17
3. School Environment 59
4. Peer Pressure. 90
5. The Impact of Modern Lifestyle 103
6. Technology. 125
7. Online Threats for Children 142
8. Video Games. 153
9. Blue Whale and Other Dangerous Games. . .160
10. Other Killer Games. 168

Disclaimer

The ideas outlined in this book have been compiled by talking to people from various sections of the society. Somewhere ancient legends have been used. The particular persons whose experiences are shared in this book have been given due credit. To bring the text in the form of a book some fictional characters have also been created. The names, places, events, etc. of the characters are imaginary and have no relation to any living or dead person, event, place or any institution.

N.K. Sondhi

N.K. Sondhi worked as a manager with Punjab National Bank for thirty years. His first book was "Management of Banking" which draws upon his experience as a Bank Manager. He then turned to fiction writing, bringing forth seen and unseen aftermaths of the partition of India in 1947 in his novel "A Cart Full of Husk" that was published in the USA. He followed it up with a short non-fiction book, "The Forgotten City of Delhi" (How the city of Delhi was founded). He wrote his next book, "A Match Made in Heaven"; A 2000-year-old love story, based on the actual life of an Indian princes Suri Ratna, who became the first queen of Korea in 48 AD and founded the Korean Kingdom. Korean people have made her Memorial in Ayodhya where they visit every year to pay their homage.

Working with young people, as he pursued social activities after his retirement, he sensed the restlessness among youngsters, facing a large number of problems due to stiff neck-to-neck competition in every walk of life. Growing use of advanced technology has further alienated them from the mainstream of the society. This led him to write a book "Know Your Worth" with the young and enterprising writer Ms. Vibha Malhotra. On public demand, a Hindi version of this book was also published under the title of "अपनी क्षमता पहचानिए".

The Advanced Technology and the Modern Lifestyle of parents have not spared even small kids. Following the footsteps of their parents, children have become high-tech children. They are busy with new gadgets then caring for their Education, Health and Physical fitness. Tacitly they are becoming the victim of online crimes, child abuses and frauds. As a result, they are losing their childhood in the rat race of modern lifestyle. This book provides some important measures for parents to save the childhood of their kids before they are lost in the wild and hostile environment of the Modernity. For children the life of their parents is a mirror for them. They need this mirror to be clean and clear. The book is published in Hindi also with title of "मत छीनो बचपन".

Acknowledgement

I sincerely thanks to Mr. S.S. Brahmi who, out of his busy schedule, had spared enough time and have taken much pain to help and guide me to improve the text of this book.

Introduction

My child is notorious, mischievous, stubborn. He is aggressive, disobedient and always in a mood of fight. He does not care for school and study. Remains busy with his smartphone. When obstructed, starts arguing.

Generally, these are some of the complaints that every parent is ready to put forward. For every single mistake, parents are quick to scold and rebuke their children but they do not try to find out the reasons for their behaviour. It is not that children suddenly develop all these traits in a day. It is a process of learning things that gradually thrives on what is available for them to learn from the people around.

In the fast pace lifestyle of modern parents, children are losing not only their childhood but it is getting worse. They are becoming insecure. Children are being deprived of good moral ethics and human values. In addition to schooling, children should be made aware of qualities such as self-restraint, service-feeling, duty-consciousness, labour, sacrifice, goodwill, dedication etc. Undoubtedly the best school for learning these qualities is their own family.

In this book, many similar issues have been discussed. They are the large part of our life which appear small and insignificant yet have great bearings on their development like tree let them grow and find their roots. No special efforts are required to resolve these issues. Only by observing certain norms with caution and practice many good habits can be inculcated in them. The very purpose of this book is to enable parents to grow their children as a good human being over and above their school education.

The Purpose of this Book

Mr. Rajan works for a private company. The day he received his son's first-year result, he was very angry. On reaching home, he began screaming at his wife. "Hey, you listen, your dear son Rakesh has failed this year also. He is not serious about his studies and never passes the final examination. You know I took a loan of eight lakhs for his admission to B.Tech. All his classmates have cleared the final exam. Only your son is waiting for some miracle to happen."

Don't blame me or Rakesh. It is because you are so arbitrary. You selected his course of study. He never wanted to go in for a science subject. You forced him to join a B.Tech Course much against his wish. And it was you who decided to take a loan. Please don't blame us for your arbitrary decisions. You wanted to be an Engineer. You could not fulfill your ambition. You want your son to do what you failed. Rajan's wife also got furious and replied in the same tone.

There is a well known saying, "As you sow so shall you reap". This is true for all parents in today's extremely competitive life. Unmindful of children's hobbies, desires, qualities, merits, demerits, or their physical and mental strengths, they are forced to fulfill the desires of their parents. Much against their own will and wish. The children are coerced to accept the decisions of parents half-heartedly. They persue what is imposed and forced on them. Most do not enjoy these decisions. Lag behind others and often get scolded. Both by parents and teachers.

In today's social environment, moral values have lost their significance. Instead, a materialistic approach is emphasized. By ignoring moral values, children can't be good human beings. They only learn how to become wealthy and powerful, to attain a high social status. They, therefore, try to get maximum marks in exams so that they can qualify as doctors; engineers etc with a lone aim just to achieve high social status. This becomes their only goal. They work hard for months and years to achieve it. Whereas on one hand, they shoulder the increasing burden of expectations from parents, teachers, and society and on the other, their mental retardation keep on increasing. When they are unable to cope with the burden, some get depressed a little few attempt suicide.

Not surprising to note that nowadays, most parents have a materialistic approach and they want their children to step into their shoes. They want their children to be well educated just to attain high positions, become successful businessmen, and earn money. With such a materialistic attitude, children do not learn the lessons of humanity. They do not try to acquire good human values. Instead of adopting the right and lawful path; they try to attain success even by unethical means. Devoid of human values. They do not try to differentiate between good and bad. The materialistic approach of parents is only because of their own self-interest. They hope their children will support them in their old age. Parents forget that children brought up with the materialistic approach of self-interest would first think of their own self benefits and losses. They would prefer to send their old parents to an old age home instead of bearing the burden of caring and their living. It might lead to the children's financial losses. There are real-life examples where we see children who are now working as doctors, engineers etc occupying high posts or doing good business, a few of them have sent their elderly parents to old age homes.

What is required today is to provide children a safe, secure and healthy environment in the family and in society, where they may get the right type of motivation, guidance, and counseling to become good people. To create such a situation, parents should be more responsible and creative. In addition to schooling, children must be acquainted with the qualities of service, emotions, duty, self-restraint, sacrifice, goodwill, dedication etc. Such an education can only be provided in the family. It is only in the family that children are educated to acquire such qualities. As individuals, we might forget what we learned in school, but we seldom forget what we have learned in childhood, from our parents. In addition to providing school education, parents should help their children to become virtuous and cultured from birth onwards. A high education does not teach people human values to become good human beings. Forget about societies or nations, children devoid of human values will not even care for their parents.

This book deals with such issues that are a part of our life but play a vital role in the personality development of children. We do not need to make a special effort to resolve these issues. Many good habits can be inculcated in children by observing and practicing certain norms cautiously. The purpose of this book is to enable parents to raise their children as good human beings, even as they undergo school education.

There may be several reasons that directly or indirectly influence the development of children, but the following issues may have more bearing on them:–

1. Family Atmosphere
2. School Environment
3. Influence of Friends
4. Impact of Modern Lifestyle
5. Technology
6. Video Games

Family Atmosphere

A family is the first school and the parents the first teachers for their children. It is in the family that children are raised and formed as human beings. Children learn the basic lessons of life from their homes. What children learn at home, they express in their behavior in society. It is, therefore, necessary for children to have such a homely environment where the atmosphere of the house is decent, calm, sweet and congenial. All members of the household respect each other, they live together lovingly, share their sorrows and support each other in times of need. Such a household provides great support in the all-round development of children. In such a family, children get adequate nutrition, security, love and all-round development. They become fearless in such an environment and continue to strive for success.

Contrary to this, if there is an atmosphere of unrest in the house every day, where there is an atmosphere of intimidation, disloyalty, arrogance, and lack of self-esteem, the children get no protection, love or encouragement. They endure harsh behavior in such conditions. Such an environment adversely affects the mental development and intellectual ability of children and they are gripped by frustration. The family is such a basic unit that helps in the development of children in a healthy environment. A family not only contributes to the overall development of children but also contributes to the development of their future.

In modern life, the joint family tradition is almost over, nuclear families are the norms. Both types of family structures have their own merits and demerits. In a joint family if parents are unable to look after the children for some reason, then their grandparents or other family members, take on the responsibility. In a nuclear family if both parents are working taking care of children becomes difficult. In such a situation servants take care of children. If the guardians are not attentive, careful and vigilant, it may create serious problems. In a nuclear family, parents feel relieved when children begin attending school, relying on teachers to look after them. But they forget that, in any school, there are good number of children in each class. It becomes difficult for any teacher to care for them individually. Therefore, the best environment for the proper development exists only in the family. The mental and physical development of children depends on the environment in their families. For Example:–

- An encouraging atmosphere at home increases children's self-confidence.
- If children observe their family members criticizing others, they learn to condemn.
- If parents are tolerant, their children will learn to be friendly.
- A happy atmosphere at home promotes the happiness and health of children.
- If struggle and conflict is a regular practice at home, children will become fearful, hesitant, hate-filled, bitter and quarrelsome.
- In the atmosphere of peace, children become moderate, patient and contented.
- If a family is disciplined, the children learn a sense of rectitude.
- An atmosphere of anger at home encourages aggressive tendencies in children.
- An atmosphere of security inculcates confidence and trust in children.
- A violent home environment makes children also violent.
- If a home is pleasant and loving, children learn to love and respect.

It is true that our lifestyles are changing very fast. We all are in a rat race to progress. Whatever the cost. Everyone wants to become wealthy and powerful. A materialistic attitude is preferred over the moral values. Everyone wants to become modern, to earn money. By hook or by crook. The people have forgotten the basic principles of human life. They adopt unethical means to serve their purpose. Such people do not realize that their children observe them minutely. They learn how to be unethical for self-interest. In such an atmosphere, what can we expect from our children? They will do as they see their parents doing. This is where we, as parents, have to act with care. Our unethical acts will drive our children to lose human values, thus becoming totally inhuman. If parents want their children to grow up as a moral istic human, they have to present a role model. they have to exhibit practical examples of ethical behavior of themselves.

They do not have to provide major examples. A homely atmosphere has a great impact on the minds of children. Matters at home have both good and bad effects. Parents must know how the atmosphere at home effects their children. The following points may help parents to understand the probable effects of home atmosphere.

PARENTS CONDUCT

Children often mimic elders, especially their parents. Children observe what their parents say and do, how they talk, what they eat and drink, how they meet with friends, and how they talk to elders. Children follow their parent's lifestyle, talking, eating habits and everything else. They are first influenced by the home environment. This is their first school. Parents are their first teachers. The life of parents has a profound effect on their children. If the parents want their children as cultured people, parents should ensure that they behave in a superior and exemplary manner. The children are clay; they can be molded the way their parents wish. Children tend to do the same as they observe their parents doing. Much like liquids they do not have any fixed shape. Liquids acquire the shape of container. That is why parents must provide good examples of their behavior for children to learn good values. Although education is important for children, human values, ethics and a good character are more important. Children learn good moral values from parents in their early life. They follow what their parents do and learn their parents' moral values. Howsoever good or bad. This does not require parents to demonstrate anything big for their children. These are only small matters that convey big lessons to be learned from their parents. For Examples:

1. Children Learn to Lie

Some time ago a man borrowed money from his friend and promised to repay quickly. But he did not return the money in time. His friend began calling him every day, asking for the return of his money. One day, his phone rang when he was sitting with his five years old son. He did not have the money. He did not want to pick up the phone. The father told his son to pick up the phone and tell the caller that his father was not at home.

Thus the father taught his five years old son to lie to avert his own trouble. Now the son learns how to tell lies. How can he believe what his father does is wrong? Unknowingly, the father taught his son an unethical lesson which son can also apply against him. Sometimes mothers also lies in presence of her children. Mothers more often than not lie to hide the mistakes of children from their husbands, in full knowledge of the children. Thus the parents teach lying to children by their own behavior.

Sant Kabir had said, "सांच बराबर तप नही, झूठ बराबर पाप" "Truth is equal to worship and lie is equal to sin". If parents teach children to lie, then you will not even have an idea that how much of parent's negligence can lead to big problems in the life of children.

As the child will grow, telling lie will become part of his nature. Then he will start lying anything and in everything. With reason. Without reason.

Wherefrom children learn the lesson of telling lies? They learn such things from the environment around, from people in neighborhood or nearby. When father himself was speaking lies, he was teaching his child to lie. It is said that "children are truthful in the mind" that children do not have this bad habit; they learn from their elders or people living nearby. Every lie is a thing which is not true. The lie is spoken when someone is cheated. The literal meaning of a lie is, "A claim that is not true and the person claiming such a claim is well aware that what he is saying is not true, yet he presents the lie as truth, means intentionally befooling others."

All of us might have heard the story of the son of the shepherd. The shepherd boy thought about harassing the villagers. Grazing his sheep in the jungle he suddenly shouted "lion is coming, the lion is coming." Hearing his screaming call all villagers rushed to the jungle to save his life. As and when they reached near the boy they found no sign of the lion. Rather the boy was laughing loudly for having befooled the villagers. There was no danger of lion and the boy was joking by telling lie. Having been cheated all the harassed villagers returned back to their work. The harassment of villagers was a matter of joy for the child. He decided to harass them again and again. Next day for the purpose of fun he cried again loudly "the lion is coming, the lion is coming." Villagers could not resist helping the boy and all of them reached to save him. It was again the matter of befooling the villagers as there was no lion. The child started laughing for having befooled the villagers again. It became his habit of making a mockery of innocent villagers. Seeing the sheep one day, there appeared a lion indeed.

The boy went to the edge of life and started calling the villagers for help. The villagers listened to his call but did not believe. They thought the boy was befooling them again. They decided to avoid his calls and nobody went to save the child. The lion not only killed the sheep but the child as well.

Truth is the mirror of life. The society recognizes a person by words of his mouth. It is, therefore, very important that parents must not, in any circumstance, lie in front of their children. A lie never goes alone; it carries with it a burden for the whole of the life. You can cheat your child or other people by untruthful talks once or twice but ultimately truth is bound to surface. Once a lie surfaces it brings a lot of defaming and a bad name in the society. A liar is not trusted by the society even if at times he speaks the truth. The most severe punishment is the fact that lier himself thinks that all other are also liers.

The impact of telling lie by children attracts more problems for them. Their classmates stop talking to them; they sever their relations from a child who is a liar. Teachers often do not trust them. Out of school friends also try to boycott a liar child. To hide a lie, ten more lies have to be spoken. There is no end to this series. People do not believe a false person even if he speaks the truth. Parents should, therefore, never ever lie in front of children nor teach them lies. Astonishingly a lier after lapse of a time starts enjoying it. He does not want to come out of it. Unmindful of severe consequences.

2. Parents' Language

About the language or voice, ancient poet Bhartrihari has written a very beautiful verse in Sanskrit:

केयूरा न विभूषयन्ति पुरुषं हारा न चन्द्रोज्ज्वलाः
न स्नानं न विलोपनं न कुसुमं नालङ्कृता मूर्धजाः।
वाण्येका समलङ्करोति पुरुषं या संस्कृता धार्यते
क्षीयन्ते खलु भूषणानि सततं वाग्भूषणं भूषणम्॥

The said Shaloka means, "the beauty of a man is not by wearing ornaments. Neither the beauty of man is due to wearing a bright necklace like silver in the neck. The beauty of the man is not by bathing, by applying sandal, nor by the use of flowers, nor by grooming his hair. The beauty of a man is by speaking a well-spoken cultured language. Jewelry is destroyed one day, but the effect of sweet, beautiful and good language always remains."

It is often seen that elders use derogatory language while talking with servants or with people of low profile. Many times men are in habit of using insulting words with women of the house. When such language is used in front of children, children learn the same type of language. Mr. Rajan cannot speak a single sentence without calling bad names two to three times. Calling bad names is his chronic habit. His conversation never ends up without calling bad names for others. His every sentence is full of abusive words. One day he invited his Boss for dinner at his home. Being punctual his boss reached his home in time. The younger son of Mr. Rajan, Ashu was present in the house. After formal welcome Rajan ordered his servant Shamu to bring a glass of water for his boss. As Shamu filled a glass of water quickly and was hurrying with a tray, his foot suddenly slipped and water spread on the table. The little boy Ashu, the son of Mr. Rajan was watching all this to happen. He instantly imitated his father and said to Shamu, "Oh you the son of a bitch are you blind? Can't you see the God of my father has come to our house? And you spoiled his clothes."

Rajan's Bose was shocked to see a small child using this kind of filthy language. Curiously he looked at Rajan. Rajan in a fit of anger started slapping his son and rebuked him saying, 'you son of a donkey, why are you calling names. You fool of the last corner must understand the situation.' Rajan was yelling.

It was enough of Rajan's boss to understand everything. When Rajan himself was abusing his son in his presence there was no fault on the part of a small child. He was just copying his father. He was well used to continuously hear his father using abusive language every day not knowing meaning of words used. In his opinion, a father can do no wrong. Abusive language of an educated person is like a stigma when commonly and frequently used in a civilized society. Children try to copy language used by their parents. If children learn abusive language from parents, there is a great possibility that they may use the same language with their friends. Consequently, it would bring bad name not only for the children but for their parents also. You may agree that such like things are like liquids. They flow from higher level to lower level.

Nowadays, it is not only the common man who uses abusive language, the veteran leaders of our country do not hesitate speaking rubbish talks on public platforms. They are also quick to withdraw their words next day. Children do not learn bad language from home only. Nowadays such derogatory language is frequently used in TV shows, in Cinemas and reality shows. Parents need to be more careful, more attentive and should seriously think before using rubbish language in presence of children. Using appropriate words is also very important for parents. It can never be other way.

Rajan's boss took a very important decision that day. He decided not to let his children keep any sort of contact with the son of Rajan. Rajan's son was denied the company of well mannered and cultured children of his Boss. Only because of his no fault. It is a known fact that speaking or listening filthy language has never been expected in a cultured society. In no way. Never ever. In spite of this even educated ones; never hesitate using such a language. Out of their ego, they recognize it to be a status symbol. In such a situation it becomes more important for parents to mind their language in front of children. For that matter even to other also.

Sometimes parents may not control themselves from using inappropriate language due to certain unavoidable circumstances and they may utter out some derogatory words unknowingly and unintentionally. For example, parents may use abusive language in following situations but it's bad affect on the minds of children cannot be ruled out:–

1. Normally a person may use abusive language which howsoever he wishes he should not had in a fit of anger. While in anger anyone may use indecent or unscrupulous language without knowing that his child is hearing carefully. If this process is repeated again and again, the child also starts using abusive language. Children keep their eyes and ears open while listening to their parents. Children may not even understand the literal meaning of their parents' words, but they remember those words by heart and may use also.

2. While expressing painful hidden emotions like pent-up emotions most people forget the language constraints and start using obscene words. If parents keep using obscene language in front of their children, their children also learn the same thing.

3. At times when parents are angry, they start abusing children directly. It has a very deep impact on their mind. A rebellion attitude in the mind of children can develop. In addition to imitating their parents, they may also directly call bad names to their classmates or other friends that may tarnish the image of the child and parents.
4. If parents want children not to learn filthy language in the first place they would have to create example of themselves. They will have to use proper, appropriate and cultured language in presence of children. In that pursuit even if they have to control their anger and emotions.

The teaching of good moral values to children is a process whose effects gradually come up from practical life. Children tend to learn bad things quickly. Therefore, it is necessary that the parental conduct is as good as possible. All the times.

3. Parents' Social Behavior

A small kid was not having any pen to write with. He requested his father to bring him a pen. Father promised but didn't bring for two days. Being stubborn the child insisted his father to fulfill his promise. One day his father gave him a very good quality pen. The child was happy to get such a beautiful pen. Out of anxiety, he started showing his beautiful pen to his all friends gladly. There lived one Mr. Jain in his neighborhood who worked in the office of his father. He knew well that the pen the child was holding is not available for sale in the market. It was a type of pens that were used by the employees of their office only. The pen given to the child was stolen by his father from his office. One day the child also stole a pencil from his school. Father knew the fact but he didn't object.

Encouraged the child started stealing. One thing from here and another from there. By his behavior father had taught a lesson of stealing to his child.

Similarly, when a father starts cheating for his self-interest then the child learns to become selfish. When the father hates others, the feelings of malice are born in the child. With squabbling habits of parents, the child starts quarrelling over the small matters. Children start learning good morals of life only by observing their parents. Display of the cooperation, empathy, friendship etc. Those who deal with respect for others, have sympathy for the poor, affection for friends and are good in social interaction, their children learn good lessons of life. Nowadays children are brought up with materialistic approach and they do not have any empathy for people or the society. Forget about the good behavior with the people of society the young generation care not behaving properly even with elders of the house.

Mr. Jack was raised by his parents lovingly. Today he works as a General Manager of a large company. His lifestyle is high profile and he always moves in high and classic society. His parents who toiled hard to get him educated are now an eyesore for him. His both old aged parents were fully depended on him and were living a fragile life in his house. Less educated parents always feared to face his modern friends. Being illiterate they were not allowed to talk or to meet high class friends of their only son Jack who never wanted people to know that his illiterate poor parents live with him. He kept his parents confined in a corner room of the house.

When Mr. Jack got the promotion, he organized a big party. The famous persons of high status of the city were invited in the party. He warned his illiterate parents not to show up in the party and ordered them to stay confined in their corner room.

It was a party full of fun, drink, and dance. People were in the mood of eat drink and be merry. All the guests enjoyed well throughout the night on this splendid occasion with every moment full of fun and fair. Meanwhile, parents of Mr. Jack were awfully hungry. They were longing for a morsel of bread. Their stomach started etching with the pain of hunger. At last, when the party was over and everyone left for their homes Mr. Jack collected some leftover food put it in a broken plate and asked his son Jony to give it to his grandparents. Master Jony the grandson was a very sensitive child. He loved his grandparents very much. He had already saved some good food for them. Disobeying his father Master Jony threw the stale food in the dustbin, washed the plate and kept it in his Almirah.

Mr. Jack was surprised to see the actions of his son who was keeping that broken plate safely in his custody. Out of anxiety, he asked him. What are you doing? Why are you keeping this broken plate in your Almirah? Master Jony replied in a low tone. Don't worry dad. It is the plate I would use to provide you with food when you get old enough like my grandparents.

It is not clear whether or not Mr. Jack was able to learn some lesson from the actions of his son but he was sure to know that children do learn what their parents do.

4. Character Building

During the fifties and sixties, there was always a compulsory lesson in the textbooks of every standard in schools. In such lessons, a summary of the life of some great person was taught to students.

Students used to learn high moral values of life from such biographical lessons of great people like Swami Vivekananda, Lok Nayak Tilak, Raja Ram Mohan Roy, Dr. Bhimrao Ambedkar, Lala Lajpat Rai, Bhagat Singh, Raj Guru, and Mahatma Gandhi etc. The elders of the house also did the work of social welfare by sacrificing of worldly things which inspired minds of children for social ethics. With the help of such lessons children used to learn moral values of life which helped them develop a high moral character.

Nowadays, politicians of criminal records have become model persons for children. Parents also vote for criminal politicians and sing their virtues. Children's character is also being spoiled by looking at the parents. In a way, this is the work of brainwashing the children. Nowadays there is no one to teach children that ordinary and simple life is the only best way for them. There may be difficulties on this path, but on this path, the future of children and society can be made safe. Parents must be the ideal for their children.

Ramesh always cursed his father. From childhood, he grew up seeing uncle Umesh, who worked with his father in his office. He lived a lavish life full of all luxuries. His house was full of all the comforts of the new age. He had everything in his house air conditioners, fridges, microwaves, televisions, and a shining car. His children had Smartphone. But there was only an old TV and a ceiling fan in the house of Ramesh. His father used the old scooter for going to his office. Ramesh's father and Umesh Uncle's salary was also equal, but Ramesh had always been longing for every necessity of life whereas Uncle Umesh's children were getting new toys and modern gadgets every day.

Watching the lavish and joyful life of the family of Uncle Umesh, he looked upon his father as a worthless person not able to manage the things for the benefit of the family. He also had a negative approach to his father who was not able to manage anything good for him. Struggling under negative thoughts he grew up and started looking for a job. Simultaneously the son of his neighbor uncle Umesh was also trying his luck for a job.

Both the youth applied for a job of salesman in a company. During the interview, Ramesh was asked to describe his family background. It is well known a fact that family background of candidates has its own weight for getting a job in a good company. It was just because of his good luck that interviewer already knew his father as well as uncle Umesh very well. Previously he was working in their office and knew about their habits also. He knew about the honesty and hardworking nature of his father and dishonest nature of uncle Umesh. He selected Mr. Ramesh thinking a son of an honest person would also have same traits. Uncle Umesh's son was rejected because of the dubious nature of his father.

What Ramesh knew about his father was his crippling financial position only. He never respected his father due to his poor financial position whereas other people respected his father due to his high character, sincerity, and dutifulness. These are things which cannot be bought with the money. Ramesh could get a job not on merits but because of the merits of his father.

Abraham Lincoln once said, *"Reputation is the shadow. Character is the tree."* Our character is much more than just our reputation, what we try to display for others to see. The important is who we are even when no one is watching.

5. House of Squabbling and Wrangling

In today's modern era, every human has everything, but there is no contentment and peace with anyone. There are some disputes and arguments in every house but where mother and father both are working the scene of that house becomes more quarrelsome. Every day's squabbling and wrangling adversely affects the development of children. In a recent survey, it was found out that 90% of children are influenced by the behavior of their parents. After constant observation of parent's behavior, a child also starts behaving like them. If the parent's behavior with each other or with the people of the society is quarrelsome the child will learn to behave in the same manner. Both at home and in the society. Due to inappropriate behavior of parents children have to face many problems in their lives. People behaving inappropriately always remain in mental stress. Due to bad behavior a person always remains stressed and tense. Similarly, when a child encounters inappropriate behavior of parents, unwanted tension is generated in his brain. The confrontational atmosphere of the house becomes the cause of fear and suspicion in the children's mind pushing them into the state of depression. Depression in itself is a big problem.

Wrangling between husband and wife is the story of every household. Squabbling parents have no concern for their children. Let the children go to hell, let them die or live, let them pass or fail, they continue to fight with each other in presence of children. When parents fight in front of children, they forget that they are messingup with their future. The childhood days are days of being happy, playful, enjoying, laughing and making merry. If the atmosphere of home is disgusting, children forget their childhood. Their innocence is lost. They become victims of a type of terror where anything drastic can happen anytime. Due to this tension, their mental development is adversely affected. An unforeseen fear in their mind is developed. This later turns to phobia due to the parents' mistakes children have to live in a wailing atmosphere of crisis where their faith and trust ends. Children living in such an atmosphere start disbelieving everyone including their parents.

According to a survey, 80 percent of children become agitated, irritable, and tense only because of the fighting problems of their parents. Their attachment to parents starts losing its ground. In such a situation, the children do not respect their parents. They suffer insecurity, start worrying about their future. Such like children become victims of inferiority complex. There is no dearth of people in this world ready to exploit the children belonging to a house full of feudalism. Such people are not other than those who have full knowledge about the house, parents and the children.

Violent behavior starts to appear in children by watching domestic violence inspired by the home atmosphere. As they grow up they also start behaving violently. Sometimes their violent behavior becomes the cause of their death. Violent children may start criminal activities. The violence in the house inspires children to commit crimes. The effect that children receive in the raw age continues for life. By watching violent activities in childhood, children also become violent.

Denise Brown has rightly said,

"Nobody believes that domestic violence kills and nobody believes it is detrimental to children. This world has got to wake up. To me, if there is domestic violence, if children see it or hear it that to me is detrimental. Batterers should not have rights to children."

6. Use of Addictive Stuff at Home

The main reason for domestic violence is intoxication. Most of the domestic violence is because of this factor only. If the parents are not alert and consume alcohol, *paan*, *beedi*, cigarette, tobacco, gutka etc in presence of children, their children also start using these items. The children feel what their parents do is good for them also without knowing that any type of intoxication may create many difficulties in their future life. Parents who are addicted to drugs, their children have to cope with the more mental, physical, emotional and health-related problems. Their children have to suffer for the consequences of the actions of their intoxicating parents. On one hand, they have to face disgrace and shame in the society and on the other hand, their friends not only begin to ridicule them they break up also. Under influence of intoxication, a father always keeps his house on tenterhooks and atmosphere of the house remains in a state of tension, uneasiness, anxiety, or suspense. Ultimately, the children of drunkards' parents become the victim of the social boycott. They are insulted everywhere. Feel guilty about themselves. Repeated insult and the social boycott may lead them to go into the state of depression. Following the footsteps of such a father, child also fall in the same line. Be sure a child is likely to copy his father in his grown-up age.

In case if an alcoholic father tries to advise his children not to drink because of its bad effects, his advice will have no practical effect on his children. This is because nobody cares for the advice of an alcoholic person. It is true in case of children also. They observed their father drinking since childhood. They would rather grow up drinking alcohol like fathers. If the father is alcoholic it takes no time his child to become alcoholic too. Once he gets in habit of addiction it becomes difficult to get rid of it throughout the life.

I Remember a Story of Childhood

There was an old widow who used to sell jaggery for livelihood. She had a son who by virtue of his bad habit would steal jaggery and eat it. This made his mother hard to run the family. She many times forbade her son from eating jaggery but every day her son used to steal and eat. The old lady always remained worried because of the bad habit of her son.

During those days there came a monk in her village who could solve all the problems of villagers. The widowed old woman went to that monk and prayed that her son has a habit of eating jaggery, which is a matter of great loss for her. She requested the monk to do something which may help her son to get rid of the bad habit of stealing and eating jaggery. The monk thought for a moment and advised the old lady to see him again after week's time. The lady went away and came back after a weak with the same request. Now again the monk advised her to come after ten days with her son. I would help your son shedding bad habit, he promised. Satisfied with the reply of the monk and having trust in him the lady went away and came again after a period of ten days. Again she was asked to come in one week's time. She obeyed the monk and went to see him after another week. Now the monk looked at the face of her son. Putting his one hand on the head of her son he closed his eyes for few moments. After a while, he opened his eyes and uttered the flowing words.

> *"Look, son, it is not good to eat jaggery more so by stealing. It is a bad habit, and, therefore, you should stop eating jaggery in future."*

The old lady was shocked over what the monk had done. If he wanted to utter these few words to her son then why he remained silent for so many days? He could have uttered these simple words on the first day itself. Why he was harassing her by forcing to visit him again and again for so many days?

The monk could well understand the confusion of the old widow. He explained her; I was not capable of forbidding your son from eating Jaggery as I was also in habit of eating jaggery. Having a bad habit myself I have no moral right to prohibit others to keep away from the same habit. If I have some bad habit how can I preach to others to shed the habit. Before advising your son I should have been first to shed my own bad habit. Had I advised your son on the first day, it could have no fruitful impact on your son. So, first of all, I abandoned my own bad habit, so that the desired impact of my advice can have its real effect on your son.

What the monk said is applicable to all parents also. As the first course of action, all the parents are required to first learn good moral values themselves. Only then they shall be able to teach their children about what is good and what is bad for them and their children would also follow them in letter and spirit. Any misconduct of parents may ruin the entire life of their children. As shall we sow so shall we reap. The best way to do a work is to start it.

7. Materialistic Approach v/s Moral Values

Nowadays, the children are being brought up in the environment and the atmosphere where total materialistic approach prevails upon the moral human values. Both mother and father are engaged in the race to earn as much money as possible. The life of both of them are so busy that neither they have the time to learn the moral ethics themselves nor do they have time to teach good moral values to their children. Instead of teaching them the qualities of becoming good human beings, they are being taught the qualities of earning more money, acquiring good fortune and becoming a Bahubali. If this order continues for a long time, then the day is not far away when the children would start treating their parents as an unwanted burden in their old age. Because of such materialistic attitude, children will forget about human values and start thinking about the life in terms of profit and loss.

Once I got a chance to visit an old age home. What I found was not believable. The son of an old aged person was a practising doctor, the son of another old age person was an executive Engineer, and the son of another old man was a big Industrialist. All of these so-called sons were earning in millions. To my utter surprise, I could not find a single old aged person in the old age home whose son was poor, unemployed, a laborer or having good income. All people in the Old age home belonged to very well-off families. Why the persons belonging to such rich families were treated as abandoned material to live a marooned life in an old age home was still a big question for me. The fact is well known to all of us. It is the same materialistic approach adopted by the siblings who have started to think in terms of loss and profit. Indeed they had learned this from their modern parents. The children are being taught to learn this very materialistic approach by parents themselves now-a-days.

The children are not at fault if they learn wrong things from the behavior of their parents. Before inculcating good habits in children, before teaching them about the moral human values and before advising children to become a man of high character all the parents must learn these human traits before teaching to their children.

8. House Discipline

Most parents presume that discipline means punishment. But the real purpose of discipline is to give right directions, to teach children to understand what is good and what is bad, to provide the proper knowledge and improving the personality of children. Discipline does not mean a licence to punish, to beat, to scold or to express anger.

All parents wish to see their children be a qualified, talented and a cultured person and their personality develop in full bloom of a high character person. Sorry to say such desire of parents can neither be fulfilled in any school, any college or in any university nor these human traits are sold in any market. For this, the parents are required to abide by self-control for which they must develop certain simple rules in the house to formulate a house discipline. Such rules will ensure that every small matter or work has its own importance.

Such rules are needed to keep the house atmosphere calm, soothing and congenial so that all the members of the family can live happily together and achieve success in their respective fields. While the elders can well understand disturbing equations of the house, it is necessary to teach the young children what is good and what is bad. The discipline of the house inspires them to behave properly. Parents shall and should be role-model for their children. Before imposing any type of discipline in the house first of all parents have to understand benefits of discipline:–

a) Discipline Accelerates Our Activities

When it is decided which work to do and when to do, where to keep which item, what to eat, when to eat, when and how long to study, where to play and how long to play, when to sleep and when to get up then life becomes easy and all the tasks start happening smoothly. The house becomes a house full of peace and happiness.

b) Discipline Helps in Concentration

If the time of study is fixed children will focus on study only. At the time fixed for playing children shall devote their energy in the playground. Similarly in every field of life children are in better position to be busy on the task at hand by following the home discipline. Gradually it becomes their habit and they will perform better in all the fields.

c) Good Habits

By observing discipline it becomes a habit to perform a particular task on a fixed time. It not only helps to finish the current task on time rather it turns into a lifelong habit of completing every work on time. This habit is a guarantee of success in life.

d) A Disciplined Life is Good For Health

The discipline of eating, drinking, walking, sleeping keeps everyone happy and healthy. There would certainly be no need to visit any doctor. On the other hand, if a person is idle not in habit of observing discipline, he would not only be wasting most of his precious time but also miss many good opportunities in life.

e) Respect

The disciplined person gets respect in the society. There is no need to make any long-term plans for home discipline. Just need to have a habit of regular and restrained life.

9. Limit of Love

Parents love their children. Every child is a lovely child for them. They are ready to sacrifice anything for the sake of their children's happiness. This love of parents sometimes exceeds its limit and out of the love for the children, they try for things which otherwise are out of their reach. They wish to fulfill all justified and unjustified demands of children at any cost. When this cycle continues for a longer time, the child becomes stubborn. In order to fulfill his stance, a child begins to adopt different kinds of tactics. Sometimes he cries, sometimes screams, sometimes declares the hunger strike and sometimes gets rude. The more stubborn children also threat to run away from the home. Blinded out of extreme love with children parents forget that they are playing with the life of their children by accepting their every unjustified demand.

Stubborn children, when grown up, go out of control. They start disobeying parents and become fearless. Consequently; a fearless child does not hesitate moving in bad company. With such an attitude, they create headaches for parents every now and then. Troublesome children thus become a matter of shame for parents making their life difficult in the society. Spoiled by extreme love most children stop caring for their parent. The notorious, ridiculous and shameful activities of such children are daily published in Newspapers. Their nefarious stories are broadcasted on TV Channels. And the punishment of their activities has to be borne by the parents. These children are the same kids who had been spoiled by parents in their childhood due to extreme love. These parents had been acknowledging their all unjustified demands without thinking about consequences. When grown up, these children get involved in anti-social and sometimes in anti-national activities. More than necessary love inspires children to get engaged in anti-family, anti-social and anti-national activities. Not surprisingly, such like children may become criminal also. Sometimes the stubbornness of children becomes the cause of their death also.

Recently, there was an accident in Delhi. A young child died only because his father fulfilled his unjustified demand.

Rich parents agreed to accept the unjustified demand of their only son and bought for him the world's most expensive motorcycle. He went on and on. One day he went on a long drive on that motorcycle with his friends during the night. The motorcycle speed was so fast that it was hard to handle. Suddenly he lost his balance. Failed to control the speeding vehicle, a terrible accident happened and the young child died instantly then and there. The repenting parents had no chance to reverse their decision. The accident, however unjust, unjustified and unjustifiable, had happened and their only son had died because they had agreed to fulfill his unjustified demand.

Before accepting the demands of children every parent must think twice about the justification of their demand.

10. Quantum of Punishment

The opinions of experts on this subject differ. According to some child specialists, children must be punished for their mistakes so that they may realize their wrongdoings and stop committing mischief in future. Children do not forget the childhood punishments and refrain from repeating same mistakes in their future life. It is said that punishment is like a teacher who enables children to distinguish what is right and what is wrong for them. Simultaneously, some other experts do not agree with the idea of child specialists. They believe that everyone is prone to committing mistakes. It is not necessary to punish for every mistake. Rather an opportunity must be given to improving. In all probability, if a punishment is necessary, it should be in proportion to the mistake. It is only enough to advise not to make further mistakes for minor mistakes. In case of some serious mistake, children should be made aware of the harmful consequences of such mistake. With a little bit counseling children may understand the situation. When the child is able to feel his mistake he may improve himself and will commit no mistakes in future.

Sometimes parents lose their patience and give excess punishment to children. With this, children lose their mental balance. Either the child may begin to disobey his parents or even kill himself. Many children commit suicide by apprehending the anger of their parents in case of getting low marks in examinations. Such types of news are published daily in many newspapers. Punishing children is not a good solution. No matter the punishment is small or big, it directly affects the mind of children and they may lose their balance of mind.

The punished, particularly repeatedly punished, children lose their balance. Become weak in studies. Gradually they decide to go against their parents. They no more wish to face their parents and rather develop a sense of rebel against them. Children get out of hand due to the corporal punishment given in anger. Love is the only way that improves even the spoiled children. The effect of any punishment given under the spell of anger never brings good results. Rather it adversely affects the minds of children. Adhering to discipline is essential, but before teaching discipline, the parents are required to present their own disciplined life in front of the children by staying in discipline themselves. The children tend to follow what their parents do. In spite of the best efforts of parents if a child continues to repeat his mistakes something sure is wrong with him. There must be some reason behind his repeated mistakes. Maybe the child is repeating mistakes deliberately to harass his parents for their strict and violent behavior. In such a situation, the parents need to evaluate their own behavior. Maybe these are the parents who can be wrong.

Remember one thing. If a child intentionally makes a mistake, time and again, it will not be an ordinary child but the master of special personality. He must have more willpower than other children. Only an intelligent child can think of new mischieves. A dull cannot. Disobedience to elders can be done only by a child who has his own ability of understanding and wants to do something different. Such children are more intelligent and understand every situation quickly. They are capable of finding solutions to their problems. Before punishing, the parents need to pay special attention to such like children. With such children, parents should neither speak in a loud voice nor should they try to manhandle. The willpower of such children is very strong. They may, in long-term force the parents for anything they wish to. They do not bother for any type of punishment for disobeying parents. There is no way to discipline them other than a shower of love, sharing their feelings and problems, counseling them with patience, sitting with them and listening to their problems and trying to solve them with their consent. Analyzing of their situation and understanding their problems can only teach them the lessons of discipline.

The purpose of punishment should never be to hurt the feelings of children. Punishment should be given in such a manner that may have a positive effect. There is always a difference between Punishment and Guidance. It should be reformative. A lesson of guidance is more effective than punishment. It is easy to make small children understand their petty mistakes but it becomes difficult to make grown-up children understand their follies.

Yes, there is a need to be more careful in case of older children. New-age lifestyles have changed the lifestyle of the children and that of their parents. It is not true that bad habits develop only in grown-up children. These may start right from childhood itself. Bad habits may develop due to some untoward incident, some unexpected event, that might have taken place in childhood. Because of such happenings, children may tend to break the rules or the discipline of the house and start treading upon a wrong path. Maybe someone is abusing children.

What should be done?

- Little children should be treated with love and older ones with friendship.
- Rules are must for a house but not for the strictness. These must be followed for the benefit of members of the family. One and all.
- Children should not follow the rules out of fear but out of respect for their parents.
- If children start scaring of their parents, then they will do something wrong.
- Parents themselves must first follow the rules of the house before they expect from their children.
- As long as children do not know the difference between right and wrong, they will continue to make mistakes. Line of distinction is very thin.
- Making children aware of the consequences of mistakes, children start working in the right direction.
- Teach them a habit of doing their own work. This will make the child self-reliant.
- If parents break the rules of the house, then they themselves should bear the same penalty which is given to children. This will encourage the children to obey the rules.

Explain the gravity of mistake to the children before awarding any punishment. Unless children are able to understand their faults no punishment would have any effects at all. After a lapse of certain period of time, the fear of punishments also vanishes from the mind of children. They become fearless and stubborn.

Please remember the home rules should be very less and very simple, these must not be ostentatious and be implemented in letter and spirit.

11. Keeping Anger in the Limit

After all out efforts, even if the child does not believe in home rules, does not listen to his parents and does not mend his habits, all put together create a situation for parents to become furious and angry. In the spell of anger, parents may commit something so serious which a child would never forget throughout his life. Later, the parents also repent for what they did in a fit of anger. It is also true that anger cannot be controlled instantly but it is only the parents who have to face the consequences of their anger outburst at a later stage. In a spate of anger if a child is beaten brutally he may inflict such serious injuries which may cost his life. Recently I happened to watch a video on YouTube where a child was scratching on the new car of his Papa with a nail. This expensive car was purchased a day before. The father wished to show his new ultra model car to his friends but before it could be done; his small child had spoiled the entire anxiety. Watching the entire outlook of the damaged car he lost his all senses, his mind went blank, he lost control over his anger and started hitting his child with heavy hands. Repeated strong slaps damaged his eardrums and the child was declared permanently deaf by doctors. Under the momentary spell of anger, the future life of the child was spoiled.

In our ancient book Bhagwat Geeta, it has been said:

क्रोधाद्भवति सम्मोहः सम्मोहात्स्मृति विभ्रमः स्मृतिभरंशाद् बुद्धिनाशो बुद्धिनाशत्प्रणश्यति

In ordinary words, man's brain gets confused due to anger. In a confused state, man cannot distinguish between good and evil, so aggressive emotions arise in him, resulting in a deadly act.

Excessive anger of parents may influence child's mind with malicious ideas that may be rebellious and revengeful. This may generate a sense of hate-inducing ideas in the mind of children and they may consider their parents as their enemies. Resultantly he may choose ways that may be wrong both for him and parents. To stop him from wrong doing parents either scold him or punish him. But how long they will scold or punish him? If the process of scolding or punishment is repeated again and again then child becomes accustomed to such scolding or punishment, consequently fear thereof vanishes from his mind. He becomes fearless of any type of scolding or punishment. It is therefore utmost important for parents to keep calm, patience and control over their anger. Anything out of control can never bring good results. Even excessive love may spoil a child. The anger out of limit can lead to even more fierce consequences.

12. Good Manners and Etiquettes

Veteran thinker Chanakya had said,

"If a child is not given his desired gift, he will cry but for a while
If he is not given good moral values of life, he will cry for a lifetime."

Good moral values of life mean good conduct, good manners and good etiquette which are important constituents of our behavior. Society recognizes us by our behavior. It is a mirror that reflects our personality. Our behavior with people of society is reciprocated in the way we behave with them. It may be well known to parents that good reputation is earned by good behavior. But in the case of children parents forget this simple rule and behave with children in derogatory manners. They also forget the difference between good and bad behavior while dealing with children. They forget that this very difference between the good or bad may make or mar the future of their children. At times parents may unintentionally show their anger, jealousness, hate, lying, abusive language, boasting, insulting elders and many other unwanted traits in front of their children. They may be doing it all unknowingly, but children take note of their every move. If this cycle persists for a long time, children also follow it. As a result, children grow older with the same instinct and start behaving vulgar. Gentle behavior has a great effect on others. People respect those who behave properly with decent manners. Any vulgar behavior of a person invites hatred and hostility only. If a highly educated person lacks good manners and etiquettes his entire education is considered worthless. Due to his vulgar behavior, people will treat him like an educated fool. On the other hand, if an illiterate person is well behaved, shows his utmost good manners and etiquettes in the society, people will have more respect for him in place of an educated person who lacks all these qualities.

We all want to see that other people should respect us. But at the same time, we forget that so-called other people would also like to expect the same respect from us. If we fail to respect other people our children are must to step into our shoes and would never show an iota of respect for others. In presence of our children, we must behave with others in a manner that we expect from them. Our good behavior with others will certainly bring qualities of courtesy to our children.

Once, King Henry IV of France (13 December 1953 – 14 May 1610) was going to Paris along with his bodyguards on the common road of Paris when a beggar greeted him with the hat off his head. The King bowed his head to his side to accept his salutation. Seeing this, a minister said to the king, you are a monarch and he is a beggar. A king need not acknowledge the greetings of poor people. In reply to the minister, the king asked him 'do you think a king should not have that much courtesy which even a gagger possesses? This is not a question whether a person is a king or a beggar; the question is whether or not a good gesture of respect shown by someone is reciprocated with the same intention. I must pay respect to anyone whosoever greets me irrespective of his status.

Any type of good manner shown by a father in presence of his children would certainly bring good results. They will learn to behave properly. Teaching good manners to children does not require any hard and fast rules. What is required is to develop a habit of behaving like a gentleman in every field. Big or small in the daily routine of life.

I would like to mention an incident that happened with me which would let us know the extent by which good manners can have their positive effects.

"I live in a flat in a Group Housing society of about 200 families. All families are well-educated philanthropic. They are either highly placed or have a big business. Every resident has his own ego and thinks himself above other people. There is a tradition in India that any person coming across is greeted by everyone by saying, Ram-Ram, Namaste or Pranam. Contrary to this ancient Indian tradition, the residents of our society, those who are wealthier expect less wealthy residents to greet them first. Most of the residents are well off and every one of them expects others to greet them first.

Children who live in this society by imitating their parents, neither pay respect to elderly persons nor do say Namaste ram-ram or pranam. But there was one child who was in habit of paying respect to all persons especially to old aged persons. Whenever I came across the said child, he would say hello to me with his folded hands. In response to his greeting, I always blessed him with good wishes and good luck. There are many more children in the society. But I have never seen any other child greeting any elderly person. It was a unique child who bowed down to everyone in respect.

One day when I was going to my home from my office, I saw a crowd of people on an intersection near the crossing of Madhuban Chowk. I came to know that a child has been hurt by a speeding car. People had gathered around him. Though a crowd of a good number of people was present on the site, no one was helping him. I recognized the child; He was the one who paid me respect every day in our society. I neither knew the name of that child nor did I know the address of his house. Since I had recognized the child I instantly got him admitted to Saroj Hospital in Rohini. I captured his photograph on my mobile phone.

I presumed the child must be living in our society. I, therefore, started searching for his parents in the society. I was trying to contact his father in the society. To my utter surprise, no resident recognized the child. Finally, a security guard of the society told that this child belongs to a poor family and his mother works in the flat number XYZ as a domestic help. The child used to come to the society every day with his mother. The owner of flat number XYZ identified the child and told that his mother lives in a slum in Rajapur. I went to the hospital with his mother instantly. The injury was not very serious but he had lost a lot of blood. I was able to provide him with timely help only because of his good manners of paying respect to everyone. His good manners had given him a separate identification. Had there been any other child of the society, I might not have been able to recognize him. I was able to recognize him by his good manners. He had a distinct identity.

I could learn a lesson from this incident that these are the manners and etiquette that establish the identity of a person. There was no identity of the children of wealthy and proud families living in the society only because of lack of their good manners and etiquettes. Imitating their parents they do not pay respect to anyone. This poor child was identified by his distinguished qualities that gave him a separate Identity. Hence; every parent should teach their children the importance of moral values through their own actions full of good manners. If the parents show their respect for others their children would certainly follow them.

Very few people show courtesy while following the rules of normal etiquettes. Most of them try to avoid the normal course of greeting behavior. Now there does not appear any practice of using words like "Namaskaar". "Namaste", or "Pranam" etc while meeting someone. When such words are said to a person he feels honored on his first meeting and paves the path for more congenial discussion. The introduction of new mediums of communication and the introduction of new technology has also reduced the level of etiquette. Today we are forgetting to use words like Namaste, Namaskaar, Thank you, Sorry etc. Today we are forgetting to use words like hi, hello, how are you, thank you, etc. Also, the practice of honoring elders, taking their blessings, and practice of taking permission of elders is also vanishing gradually. The importance of respectable words must be explained to children by their parents so that they may develop positive qualities in their personality right from childhood.

13. To ERR is Human

Committing mistakes is normal for all of us. There is no man in this world who never committed any mistake. Children are also not exception, they also commit mistakes. It is normal for them. What is important for a parent is to understand the types of mistake and reasons thereof. It is very common for children to commit mistakes in matters associated with studies, homework, food or games. There is nothing serious as it is the daily routine for them. After giving a little bit of counseling small children may stop committing such minor mistakes in the future. A serious problem arises when parents themselves become part of their wrong doings and start assisting in the wrong actions of their children. Knowingly or unconsciously when a child steals, lies, skip from school, and snatches away the things of other children, most of the parents come to their rescue. They say, our child is yet very young and he is not able to understand what is good or what is bad. Once grown up he may learn good habits. Parents mostly forget that the bad habit learned in childhood becomes a permanent part of their life. Seldom they are able to shed wrong things learned during their childhood. Ignoring childhood's bad habits can ruin not only the lives of children but can create serious problems for parents as well. Some of the bad habits fall into the category of crime. Ignoring such mistakes of children is a mistake that can ruin not only the lives of children but also of the parents. There are some mistakes that happen in the category of crime.

It is understandable to ignore the minor mistake by the parents. This can be out of their love and affection for children. For minor mistakes punishment, if any, should also be minimal. A major punishment for a minor mistake may develop a sense of fear in the mind of children. After getting scared of parents children may start hiding their all mistakes, hating parents and his mental status may get unstable. In such a condition if the child comes into contact with some outside person who may exploit and abuse him showing artificial love for him. Maybe this outsider is a criminal resultantly the child may also grow up learning criminal activities in his company.

In the normal course of life, parents start punishing children before children are able to realize their mistake. The first step for parents should be to make children realize their mistakes. Children remain unaware of the consequences of their mistake without realizing it or without knowing reasons thereof. Before punishing the child, it is necessary for the child to get to know the seriousness his mistake and its aftermath. On the contrary, the parents put different kinds of restrictions on their children to control them. As a result, the children feel to be more uncontrollable and go out of control. It should be very clear in the minds of children what they are being asked to do and if not done accordingly what could be the consequences. As long as the things are not very clear in the minds of children they may continue to make mistakes.

It is most essential that parents should never try to conceal mistakes of their children. This encourages children to commit more serious mistakes. Slowly, the child would start doing very grave mistakes which may be difficult for parents to set right. Such mistakes can be criminal in nature and may attract legal difficulties. Once the law comes into the picture most of the children are likely to become criminals. It then becomes difficult to come out the world of crime. Such children may cause more harm to parents and society.

14. Comparison of Children

Not all children are equal. Two children born in the same house can be completely different. A child can be smarter in sports; the other child can be skilled in music or painting. If one becomes a criminal then the other can become a Police Officer. This is not a game of luck. It depends on what the parents contributed to the development of each child.

More often than not happens is that parents expect them to do better instead of praising children's accomplishments already achieved. They start embarrassing their children by comparing their performance with other intelligent children. With the result, parents create an inferiority complex in their minds. The child with an inferiority complex always thinks others to be superior and starts lagging behind them. Ultimately he becomes a victim of mental torture. If such comparison is done with the sister or brother of the child it creates an atmosphere of enmity between them.

Ramesh's son Rahul was working hard for his Class X exam day and night. Nor did he had the senses to eat, to play; his only aim was to get maximum possible marks in the examination. With his hard work and dedication, he scored 80% marks in the examination. He gladly reached home and wanted to give good information to his parents. His father was not at home, he showed his test results to his mother. On seeing the result card his mother not only appreciated him but also loved him passionately. Meanwhile his father Mr. Ramesh also reached home. He looked at the exam results with a cursory look and kept aside. After keeping the result card aside his father didn't utter a single word of appreciation for his son. Surprised by the behavior of her husband Rahul's mother asked him to speak something in praise of his son who scored very good marks in the examination

Furious with anger Mr. Ramesh looked on his wife with red eyes and asked, why should I appreciate him? He has spoiled my reputation. Mr. Suresh who works as my assistant in my office, his son Nitin has scored 95% marks in this examination. He is my helper and I am his boss. I have been insulted in the entire office because of my son. Rahul immediately started screaming and crying and ran away from the home listening disgusting words of his father. After passing the examination with good marks, Rahul was hoping that he would be praised at home; his father would love him and would increase his enthusiasm. But everything went wrong. Neither was he praised nor received any respect; rather he was insulted by his father.

When Ramesh realized that Suresh's son Nitin had copied it in the examination, he regretted profoundly but now he had lost the chance. It was too late for him to realize his mistake. Now Rahul hated his father. He made friendship with Nitin who was in the bad habit of cheating everyone. In the company of Nitin, Rahul also started following his habits. Just think why this happened? The parents raise unnecessary expectations of their children.

Maybe the parents want to fulfill their suppressed desires, which they failed to accomplish themselves, through their children or they wish to pretend to be the best in the society out of their inflated ego.

Children should always be complimented for their good performance and not to despise them. Inspiration to do good work comes from praising and encouraging the children. If children are compared only to tell their weaknesses, then gradually the children start to understand that other children are better than them and they themselves are not worthy of anything. When such thoughts start coming from the minds of children their educational and personality development is adversely affected. The continuous comparison becomes a burden for them and the personality of burden-laden children can never grow.

Instead of comparing children the parents should try to understand their problems with love and affection, start talking and discussing with them about their problems and help them in finding a suitable solution.

15. Become a Role Model for Children

By just reading the lines mentioned about does not help to create a good family atmosphere. It requires a lot of other efforts to be done. Every family enjoys its own reputation in the society from generations to generations. As such every family has its own perceptions, thoughts, religious belief and some families also have traditional customs. Such old-time traditions of a family have long time influence on the development of children. Children spend only 4-5 hours in their school and maximum time in their respective homes. The children tend to fall behind the race in the competitive life where families keep them pressurized to perform traditional rituals or customs. When children find it difficult to compile with old-time orthodox traditions of family they lag behind the race of modern age. In such a situation, the responsibility of the children's failure falls on the parents. Bad traditional customs or social practices are great enemies for children. For the proper development of children it is, therefore most necessary that the atmosphere of the house should be friendly, congenial, peaceful and co-operative. Creating such a beautiful atmosphere of the house is the first duty of every father.

Psychologists believe that children in every home follow the domestic environment in which the father's role has special significance. The effect of the father's lifestyle, his thoughts and his habits is the highest in children's lives. Father is the ideal of children and most children follow their father. If there is something wrong in the lifestyle of a father, children would grow with same faulty lifestyle. The children of an ideal father grow happily living a prosperous life and gain competence to face every challenge of life.

The good family environment does not depend on the behavior of parents alone. There are so many other elements that have an impact on creating the home environment. As an example, images on the walls of the house have their own influence on the children. If such pictures are of obscenity, eroticism, cheap forms of charming beauty or cinema actresses, people smoking cigarettes or drinking alcohol, definitely the environment of the house will become contaminated, which will have a contaminating effect on the lives of children.

On the contrary, if the walls of the house are decorated with images or pictures of great people, brave youths, patriots and known social workers it would have a special effect in the formation of children's character. Otherwise, in the families, where there is conflict or fight, there are drinking or smoking habits, in the families where children are scolded/beaten and servants are mistreated, no power on the earth can save children of such families becoming evil and ruthless.

Dressing sense of the family members conveys an indirect effect on the mind of children. Wearing sexual dresses, using aromatic creams, wearing ultra modern makeup by the family members would certainly attract children towards perverted habits and criminal activities. Nowadays, the Newspapers are full of misdeeds by minor youths. Just think of those parents whose children are convicted for heinous crimes. They are neither able to stand by their children nor able to face the society.

It is the rule of nature. To receive something one has to sacrifice many things. Parents have to sacrifice a lot for bringing up their children as a respectable human being.

School Environment

In the earlier times, the schools functioned as a nation-building institutions where teachers were known as Gurus and students as pupils. The Guru used to give full support for all round growth of his disciples without any self-interest. In return, the disciples used to devote everything to their gurus. Over the time, the nature of schools changed and today the schools have transformed into a money-making industry. Earlier, only coaching centers were considered as a means of earning money. But nowadays schools are run like a corporate company, whose only aim is to earn money. New excuses are framed to charge maximum fees from the students. Schools are designed to look very attractive with air-conditioned classrooms, computers, digital systems, and all this is used as an advertisement to get maximum enrollment of students. To make maximum money, school management adopts all kinds of tricks. Even teachers are not appointed on the basis of merits and qualifications. Less educated people are appointed on a low salary. In order to defy the rules, teachers are paid more salary (as required by the law) through cheques but sufficient cash is collected before handing over the cheque to them. Only God knows how much attention is paid to the education and safety of children in such schools.

All Parents, whether poor or rich, want to enroll their children in a good and a famous school. Without caring for the cost of education they wish to see the improved future of children. The professional schools take full advantage of the feelings of parents. As such parents should be very careful in selecting a right school. Almost half of the educational institutions in the country have got the protection of political leaders directly or indirectly. Most of the owners of these schools are associated with some political party. In such schools, no proper action is taken in case of any miss happening with students.

In our country, schools have been opened in every corner and on every street, which are run by private people. Many such schools are not even recognized. Some of such schools are working from residential premises to cater to the needs of the people of the lower segment of the society. It is only middle-class people who have to face many admission problems for their children. They want better schools for their children which are too expensive and beyond their financial capacity. Government schools are good for nothing for them. In the absence of an effective National Education Policy different kinds of schools are functioning in our country like:–

1. Government Schools

State schools are governed by the government where bureaucracy dominates the system. The biggest hazard of bureaucracy is that left hand does not know what the right hand is doing. Though the fee in state school is very nominal, but they lack in terms of structure and facilities. There is no second opinion that teachers of government schools are well educated and trained, but they have no responsibility towards education of students. Study or not is student's choice. Teachers in state-owned school least bother about personality uplift students. Classrooms of govt. schools lack facilities in comparison to privately owned schools.

2. Public School / Private School

The name of the public school is confusing because every government institution is called a public institution. From this point, it seems as if public schools are government schools. But, in contrast, public schools are completely private, which are managed by private people. There are some aided schools which get financial support from the government. Financially aided schools have to go according to government rules, whereas public schools are managed by private people.

Business minded people have made schools a source of wealth earning. In order to earn even more money, they select famous names for their schools which look more attractive, like International School or Global School but these are all private schools. Just as industrialists earn profits by investing in the industries, in the same way, rich people open schools to earn money by investing in schools and not for improving the education level of the country or for the development of children. Parents should, therefore, pay special attention to selecting a proper school for their children.

Merits and Demerits of Government Schools

- In Government schools, a very nominal fee is charged which facilitate poor people to admit their children in Government Schools. Most of the children in India are studying in government schools only.
- In Government school minimum possible facilities are provided to students which are basic in nature. There remains no arrangement for the overall development of the students, such as sports, fitness system, tournaments, etc. There is also a problem of cleanliness and drinking water in these schools. The condition of the toilets is also not suitable.
- The teachers of government schools are trained but apart from teaching, many other tasks are imposed on them by the government because of which they cannot pay full attention to the education of children. As such the children of these schools fall behind at the time of any competition.
- The courses of these schools are in accordance with prescribed rules.
- The building of the school and the furniture of the classroom leaves much to desire.
- Students have to do their own transport arrangements to attend school.

Merits and Demerits of Public/Private School

- By the look of their buildings, they appear to be a five-star hotel. The parents get fascinated by seeing the building.
- Air-conditioned classrooms, digital boards, beautiful desks, and glazed surroundings.
- Playgrounds, all facilities, children's food arrangements and emergency services.
- Admission is very difficult. Admission is done through the examination of children, parental interview, and donation power.
- Annual fees can range from 50,000 to 2 lakh.
- Their own norms of Fees and Curriculum Course.
- Most teachers work on a contract basis and are not paid salary according to state rules.

Parents send children to school for education since they wish them to grow up like a good human being after completing their schooling. This passionate emotion of parents drives them to search for a very good school even if it is a very expensive one. Education in our country was considered as a noble cause, not a business. Till the time education was deemed to be a noble cause, the schools were considered like temples. The safest place for children. Now education has become a business, a shop with a sole motive of earning maximum profit. Education has become a commodity of profit and loss for people now. The real purpose of education has gone into oblivion; it is neither understood by teachers nor the parents. After admitting the child in the school parents feel having done their duty and teachers are satisfied with imparting merely bookish knowledge to them. Nobody is bothered to know what exactly children learn in their schools.

The real purpose of education is the entire development of life. According to Swami Vivekananda, "It is the work of education, to direct the completeness which is present in the sub-form of man." According to Plato, "The aim of education is to make the body and soul more and more as complete with beauty and development as it can be." According to Mahatma Gandhi, "If a person wants to learn, every mistake can give him some education."

According to the above great persons, a school should be the best institution in the country. But the real condition of schools in our country is well known to all of us. The condition of government schools is such pitiable that the managers, teachers, and principals of these schools are not ready to teach their children in a government school. All of them prefer to send their children to private or public schools. Where there is a will there is a way. Where there is no will there is an excuse.

CHILD SAFETY IN SCHOOL

Every person wants good education for his children and also sends them to expensive schools. Once a child is admitted to a good school, parents feel relaxed and rather go to slumber. They are least bother to know what is happening with their children in the so-called expensive school. They wake up out of their slumber only when something serious happens with their children on the school premises. Parents need to be ever alert if they wish protection of children. Parents are required to take care of many things like:–

1. Distance from Home to School

Do not select a school that is very far from the home. In pursuit of a good school, (normally expensive schools are considered to be good schools) do not admit your child to a school located far away from your residence. It would take more than sufficient time to reach school and back to home. With the result, children will be left with no time spare for their study, homework or for playing. Moreover, it would badly affect their health also. God forbid if something untoward happens with the child, it would certainly not be possible for parents to reach school instantly.

2. School Related Information

The parents are pleased with the shining building and a big name of the school. They do not try to collect information about the so-called best school selected by them. Collecting important information about the school is very essential for the parents at least some of the following information:–

3. Environment

The school environment is very important for the safety of children. The school environment should be such that there is no fear in the mind of children. This fear is not related to the study but the fear generated out of the misdeed or misbehavior by school staff. Afraid of the strict behavior of school employees children tend to obey their every order good or bad. This is the element of fear in the mind of children due to which they become the victim of sexual abuse. The parents should, therefore, must visit the school from time to time to know about the environment of the school.

4. Who is the Owner of the School?

What we know is that the Principal is the overall in-charge of the school. In fact ownership of schools nowadays vests with some rich man or an Industrialist and the Principal is just an employee like other employees of the school. Like other employees, he is also bound to obey the orders of the owner. In such a situation parents must know who is the owner? Is the school being run by some educational institution or by some Industrialist? In case the owner is any Industrialist parents should be more vigilant because the aim of any Industrialist is to mint money and not to impart education. In order to earn more and more money, he would never care for the safety of children.

5. C.C.T.V

The installation of CCTV Camera in school should not be a matter of show off only. It should serve the real and required purpose. Mostly for saving money CCTV Cameras are not installed in washrooms, gallery, playgrounds and on children's way. All these places are very important for the safety of children which are ignored to save the money. Parents must take up this issue with school management.

6. Emergency

Parents should find out whether there exists a system to deal with emergencies?

7. Responsible Officer

There should be an officer on every floor of the school responsible for the protection of children.

8. School Buses

Whether the school buses embark or disembark children within the school gate or outside the gate.

9. Whether there is a responsible employee on the school bus, to ensure that every child safely reaches school and goes back home.

10. Medical Facilities

Medical facilities in school are for name sake only. Usually, the doctor does not remain present in school for a full time. He is called by phone only when needed.

NOT ONLY STUDY, CHILDREN CAN DO A LOT MORE IN THEIR SCHOOLS

What is said above, are the things that are apparently visible, can be seen, checked, felt and tested. But still, children remain busy doing a lot more activities in schools about which parents are ignorant. They come to know about these activities if something wrong happens with children. Best arrangements of study are made in most private schools nowadays. It is therefore that the classrooms of these schools are called smart classrooms which are fitted with the latest gadgets of modern technology like computers, laptops, videos, DVD, and smart boards etc. All students complete their study using new technology equipments. They need not taking notes nor do they need to write anything in classrooms. Simply copy and paste on the laptop, smartphone or any other device and finish class studies. Go home and memorize lessons, do homework through the equipment. Neither they need to ask teachers any question nor are teachers required to answer any question. Whatever students wish to ask they must ask their system. This arrangement does not give children an opportunity to overcome their doubts from teachers face to face. Children are forced to solve their problems on the laptop. No one is aware of which site the children may visit while searching for their educational problems. Some sites may spoil the future of children. And that is happening also.

Children of rich families are accustomed to luxurious life. Their parents often arrange big parties at home to celebrate one or the other occasion. Cigarettes, tobacco, alcohol etc. are used openly in these parties. Children try to follow what they see. When they do not get these things, they try to find out their alternatives. Some time ago some children were caught at the Noida School while smelling Erasing Fluid. This fluid contains some toxic contents. The event is small but its bad effect is very serious. When the pressure of studies increases on children and parents expectations also increase in the same proportion the children are gripped in a state of tension. This tension affects so badly their mind that they go in a state of doldrums. They are not able to think about themselves. In such a situation, the children of rich families suggest them a simple way of getting rid of stress. By seeing regular use of the drug by parents they themselves are addicted to drugs now. They, therefore, motivate other stressed children to use drugs. Alcohol is necessarily not the only drug that is used to feel high. There are many other low-cost alternatives freely available in the market.

There are many things readily available in every house also at all times. Like cough medicines. There are some ingredients in cough medicines that produce intoxication. Regular and frequent use of cough syrup leads to addiction. If children are using cough syrup repeatedly by pretending to be suffering from cough, then parents should understand that there is something wrong. Likewise, there can be many other items available in every house that children may use for intoxication.

The age of 5-15 years is very fragile. At this age children have a strong desire to learn something new, and experiment. These children, standing at the threshold of puberty, want to do a lot. In this age, children come in contact with society, outside their home, where there is no restriction of domestic rules or discipline. At the same time, they get new friends in school. They do not care about the money they spend. They tend to do something new every day. In this age, children want to live their life in their own way. They think they have grown up. They can choose their own path. By meeting with other children in school, they also adopt their mannerisms some of which are against the rules of the house. If the parents try to stop, children may start rebelling. In such circumstances, parents should try to handle the situation with great patience. Otherwise, children under the influence of other children (who themselves are minor), can go astray. Choosing a wrong path they may become victims of bad habits in which the worst thing is to become drugs addict.

It is not necessary that the addictive goods are found outside the house or school only. There are many such things which cause intoxication and are available not only at home but in schools as well.

Things which are available in schools:–

Glue

It is wrong to say that gum is used only to paste something. There are certain types of gums, used in garages, furniture shops, and tire repairing shops which contain chemicals that produce intoxicating effects. Their highly inflammable and evaporating contents are used by children like intoxicating material. They inhale it after pouring this chemical on a handkerchief and later start sucking that napkin. Within a few minutes, the innocent face of the child appears horrible with the effect of addiction. Eyes start inflating.

Erasing or Correcting Fluid

This white color chemical works to remove words written on paper. Children use it to erase the mistakes of their handwriting. At any stationery store, it is available at very low prices. Its intense odor not only erases the words written on paper, but it also removes memories from the human brain. By a stint of its smell children start dancing as if they are heavily drunk. Its effect is so dangerous that it can badly affect the whole system of the body by infecting the entire blood. Copying each other, children use it first for attaining happiness and later they fall victim to addiction. In 2011, some children were caught on a CCTV camera while using it in a well-known school in Noida. A PIL was filed in Delhi High Court and it was requested to ban it. Consequently, the Delhi government had banned its sale but it is still easily available in the open market.

This is only one example but there are a number of other such substances easily available in schools or outside of schools, which children use for intoxication. Some of these substances are used in smoking, some by smelling, some other by inhaling which include a particular type of glue, lighter gas, markers, paint thinners etc. All these substances become volatile at room temperature. Children snort them or put them on a napkin or cloth and breathe repeatedly. There are other such substances also which are used for spraying like mosquito sprays, fly sprays, deodorants and even hairspray. All these items contain intoxicating elements and their frequent use by children may become a cause of intoxication.

There are innumerable substances which are introduced to children by car drivers, peons, school staff, gatekeepers, and by their rich friends. At last but not the least there is internet from where children may get all types of information as per their requirements. The sad and sordid part of the story is that these drugs are available everywhere at very cheap prices without any restriction. Even so many substances are found in every house.

It is true that cases of child addiction are increasing in schools. The problem is that there is no narcotics policy related to protecting children in India. Neither is there any such program by the government to warn or alert the parents about this danger nor any guidelines are provided to school management or parents. Parents are, of course, an ignorant stuff on this regard. Of course, there is a law called "Narcotic Drugs and Psychotropic Substances (NDPS) Act 1985 for punishing children in the crime of drug possession. But there are no health centers for the prevention of Substance Drug Abuse of Children. In rural areas, the situation is even worse.

How to Save Children?

Before that it will be too late for the parents to take command, they have to be aware and alert. The problem cannot be solved by giving punishment to children only. Maybe, after getting the punishment, the children start using more and more intoxicants. First of all, parents need to find out the tacit reasons for which the children use drugs.

We cannot say there is a definite reason for children to get addicted. According to situations and circumstances, the reason may ditter from child to child. The parents have a great misconception that the school life is very easy as children do enjoy every minute of the time spent in the school. According to them, children have to do nothing except to study, playing, eating and enjoying a worry-free life. But this is not true in today's environment. There can be many difficulties in children's lives; they also have to face stress and difficulties. To get rid of their stress and difficulties they may take help of drugs. There can be a number of reasons for them to start using drugs in school life:

1. **The Influence of Friends:** If the neighbor's child is using a drug without knowledge of parents, make sure the day is not far away when your child also may fall in the grip of his habits. Apart from this, other children also provoke them to be brave and to behave like a grown-up man. This type of provocation is taken as a challenge. In order to prove brave and a grown-up man, every child easily accepts such challenges. Together, the children's group starts enjoying drugs.

2. **Pretentious to be Brave:** Everyone knows that after taking intoxication, everybody starts to think of himself as brave. Even children are not untouched by this habit; they also become victims of this disease to prove themselves brave.

3. **Learning Problem:** The environment of throat cut competition is adversely affecting most of the children. Due to

the increased pressure of studies; the children cannot concentrate on any subject. They need to focus their attention. There are certain medicines available in the market like Ritalin and Adderall which are used by children to get mental stability in order to concentrate on their study. But more and longer use of such medicines makes them drug addicts.

4. **The Behavior of the Parents:** If the parents or other members of the family use drugs at home, the children start following them.

5. **Boredom**: When a child is bored, he is eager to do something new. The easiest means of removing boredom is to get rid of it and the simple way of fun is the addiction.

6. **Depression or Mental Confusion**: When a child is depressed, he loses his interest in any type of activities. Not being able to stabilize mental status children start taking drugs.

One third of their lives people spend in boredom without knowing what exactly it is.

It is a disease.
A serious one.

A peculiar quality of boredom is that once a person starts getting bore, after lapse of some time, he starts enjoying. He does not want to get rid of it. He does not want to come out of it.

Boredom leads to depression which ultimately more often than not leads to suicides. Menace of drug is an alternative to young mind. They are an easy prey.

Symptoms and Signs of Addiction

To keep children away from addiction, parents need to be alert all the time. The behavior, body gestures and habits of addicted children start changing. Parents are required to take notice of such changes. There may be a number of signs which indicate drug use by children. Some of which can be as follows:–

- Eyes are dilated and get red.
- The child becomes moody.
- Child behavior changes.
- The child stops chasing his hobbies.
- Starts lying and stealing.
- Makes new friends.
- Getting annoyed over petty matters.
- Use more aromatic chemicals to hide the smell of drugs.
- Being careless or depressed.

There can be other indications also. If parents are careful and alert, they can recognize any type of drug signs. There may be severe consequences of being addicted in childhood. This can harm the liver, kidney, lungs of the children. Children become mentally weak, start forgetting things, their behavior becomes fierce and aggressive. They remain mentally disturbed. Gradually they start losing friendship with other children. Without friends, they start feeling loneliness which has its own bad effects.

We have been talking about the intoxicants which are easily available either at home or in schools which are also available in a nearby stationery shop at a lower cost. But according to some doctors working in schools, children of the age of 12-15 years have started using high-drugs like cocaine, heroin, LSD, Cannabis etc. On being caught these children are just warned or suspended from school for a few days as a punishment. At the most, these children are sent for counseling by school management. About a decade ago, children used to smoke cigarettes or drink beer, but recently their habits are getting worse. The root cause in the first instance may be the carelessness of the parents or parents themselves using drugs in presence of children. The influence of outside people or schoolmates comes later on. First of all, parents have to abstain from alcohol before restraining their children. Soon after finding the signs of intoxication by children parents should get alert immediately. This does not mean start hitting, beating or scolding them. First of all, they should try to find the reasons. It requires a great amount of patience and peace in order to know the mind of children. The best way is to discuss with children about their problems with love and teach them to be able to distinguish between good and bad. Teachers in schools are mostly busy to complete the curriculum. They do not have the time or inclination to teach about character building. It is, therefore, more important for parents to take initiatives to develop good moral values in their children.

It would not be proper to blame only teachers in this regard. Nowadays, the trend of children is increasing towards social media and not for the study of monotonous curriculum in the classroom. Digital and internet topics have been discussed separately in this book in detail. It is tried to explain here that all these new devices of advanced technology are creating problems for children. Children are more eager to know what is going on in their chat, what's new on Hottestar, What Does Whats App group is discussing about? Using digital platforms children are trying to know which they must not know at this tender age.

TRAFFIC ARRANGEMENT

Parents are happy once their child is admitted to a famous school. They proudly declare that our child is admitted to the best and most expensive school in the city even if the school is located outside the city miles away from home. In such a situation, parents have to make special efforts to arrange for a car, a van or a bus for commuting children to schools and back to home. Here also the so-called high-class schools have their upper hand. Schools take a loan from banks to purchase the buses and for repayment of the loan; they charge every penny from parents with interest. Thousands of rupees are collected per month in the name of transport and the parents happily pay it. But they do not try to know if the bus in which the child is being sent to school is safe or not. It is very important to note a few things:–

- If you are going to drop your children please do not leave the children outside the school gate, but leave them inside the school.
- The Identity Card issued by the school should always be with the child.
- Make sure your child knows his full name, your full name, home address, your phone number, home phone number.
- If the child is too small this information should be available in his school diary. Keep in mind that such information should not be written on the child's uniform or on his bag. Naughty elements can not only take advantage of this information but can also exploit your child.
- If the child uses the school bus, parents are satisfied with the safety of their children. This can also be a misunderstanding among parents. Recently there have been some incidents

School Environment

with children, either on school buses or by employees working on school buses.

- All the buses used by schools are not owned by them. Some buses are also taken on the contract basis. First of all, find out who is the owner of the bus? It is very easy to get this information. You can get this information immediately by sending an SMS from your mobile phone to the Transport Department. This information can be obtained in the following manner:

   "To send SMS on mobile phones, you have to type VAHAN followed by the space then type the full registration number of the vehicle without space and send this message to 7738299899. In just a few seconds the name of the owner of the bus will appear on your phone."

- If the owner of the bus is a private person then get information about his contract with the school. If the owner does not have a contract with the school then the school can refuse to take any kind of responsibility in case of an eventuality.
- You need to be on alert even if the ownership of the bus is with the school because these buses are purchased with a bank loan and driver and conductor are not appointed by schools. If they are not on the payrolls of the school, the school may refuse to accept any responsibility.
- The bus driver should have a valid driving license. Similarly, the conductor should have a valid badge.

As a parent, you have the right to know all this and you must also know. If any doubt, please read the instructions issued by the Central Board of Secondary Education.

DIRECTIONS BY THE CENTRAL BOARD OF SECONDARY EDUCATION RELATED TO THE TRAFFIC OF CHILDREN BY SCHOOLS

According to orders of the Honorable Supreme Court of India, the Central Board issued these instructions to the Principals of all public, private and aided schools on 23.02.2017. Those schools that do not follow these instructions can end their accreditation. This is only possible if parents are alert and careful. These instructions are being given below for parents' information. Please read carefully. If any of the schools is not following them, take appropriate action against them. Children will continue to be exploited if parents are silent. The orders related to the school buses are as follows:–

1. **External Color of Buses:**

   a) Buses should be of yellow color and the name of the school on both sides of the buses should be written in bold letters so that they can be easily identified.

   b) "School bus" should be written in bold letters in front of the school bus. If the bus has been taken on contract and its ownership does not vest with the school the words "ON SCHOOL DUTY" should be written on the bus in bold letters.

   c) The complete address of the bus driver, license number, and badge number should be available on the bus. In addition, the address of the owner of the bus and phone number of the school should be written on the bus. The number of helplines of the Transport Department should be clearly written on both sides of the bus. This number should be written in such a way that it is easily visible to the general public and to the people sitting in the bus so that the information can be immediately reported to the school management/police / other related officers in case of emergency.

2. Inside the Buses

a) The windows of the buses may be opened above the top and they are covered with rods and they have gauze wire.
b) There should be a system of locking the doors of the bus
c) It is the responsibility of school management that every bus has an emergency exit door.
d) The buses should have a speed control system and the speed of the bus should not exceed 40 km. per hour.
e) It is the responsibility of the school to have at least two fire extinguishers of ABC Type ISI Mark 5 Kg on each school bus. One of which should be in the driver's cabin and the other must be near the emergency door. Training should be given to the driver, conductor and lady assistant/guard to use these devices.
f) For the safety of the children, the seats of the school bus should be made of the material which cannot be used for fire.
g) Must have GPS and CCTV in every school bus. The owner of the bus has the responsibility to ensure that GPS and CCTV are operable at all times.

3. Bus Staff

a) Each school should appoint a traffic manager who will be responsible for the safety of every child traveling in school buses. The name and phone number of this traffic-manager should be written in thick and bold letters inside and outside of each bus.

b) The bus driver must have a valid driving license and he should have at least five years of experience of driving buses.

c) The bus conductor should also have a valid license. His qualification and his duty should be in accordance with the provisions of rule 17 of the Motor Vehicles rules.

d) It is the responsibility of the school to appoint an assistant/guard on every school bus, who takes full care of the safety of children during the journey. Apart from this, he or she will have to help children for embarking and disembarking the bus.

e) School management should make sure that at least one such parent is ready to go with the children on the bus, who can monitor the driver, conductor, and other school staff. This will ensure that the rules of safety of children are being properly followed and the bus driver is running the bus carefully.

f) In any case, no other person should be allowed to travel on the school bus except the bus driver, conductor, assistant woman and a guardian.

4. Facilities in Bus

a) First Aid Box in the school bus and drinking water should be arranged.
b) There should be an arrangement of keeping school bags either under the seats or any other suitable place.
c) There should be arrangements of alarm bells or sirens in the school bus so that everyone can be informed in emergency time.
d) There should neither be curtains in school buses nor should the glasses be fixed with the film.
e) Proper lighting should be arranged in school buses.
f) The activities within the bus should be clearly visible from the outside while on the road.

5. Permits

a) No school will use any bus or another vehicle which does not have permits from state transport.
b) According to the Motor Vehicle Act 1988, bus or other vehicle and passengers' insurance is necessary.
c) Driver's medical examination and his eyes should be checked every year. Every year, the relevant medical certificate will be presented to the authorized officer.
d) The school can not appoint a driver who has more than two challans in one year, whether on account of violation of red light, high speed, lane -driving or even if an unauthorized person is allowed to drive.
e) To run a school bus or a vehicle, the school can not appoint the driver whose single challan is due to running the bus

dangerously or under the code of the Indian Penal Code, under 279,337,338 and 304A or under POCSO ACT.

f) The driver needs to wear a uniform of gray color set by the State Transport Department, on which his name and the name of the owner of the bus should be written on a badge.

g) The school bus can only be run by a person who has a valid badge of public service vehicle issued by the state transport department on which his photo is attached.

h) If the age of traveling students is less than 12 years then their number should not be more than one and a half times of the available seats. Students aged 12 years of age will be considered as adults.

i) The fitness certificate shall have to be procured every year for school bus according to the Motor Vehicle Act 1988.

j) If the drivers or schools violate motor vehicle act 1988, violate any of rules related to them, violate any of court orders or violate Central Board's directives they will be prosecuted under the law.

k) If the school hires a bus then the school will have to make a written contract with the owner, whose copy should be always with the driver all the times.

l) The full information of all the students traveling on the bus should be available with the bus driver, in which the names of the children, class, blood group, bus stop, and bus routes must be clearly written.

m) If the contractual bus is used, then the owner will have to give the bus related information to the nearest police station and the concerned traffic police officer and give the full name and address of the driver.

n) The driver cannot use mobile phones while on the bus, and neither can talk to students or other staff more than needed.

6. The Responsibility of School for Buses

a) It is the duty of the school to ensure that all the doors are closed properly in Moving Bus.
b) School buses should stop at the fixed place only at the fixed stops.
c) The school is responsible for the safety of children while getting in and getting out of the buses.
d) The bus will not move when children are getting in or getting out of the bus.
e) New training should be given to school bus drivers twice a year in order to increase their skills.
f) A driver should not be allowed to drive the school bus in a state of intoxication. In case of doubt, the school authorities will have to carry out a medical examination of the driver and, if found guilty, will be required to take action against them, even action will be taken to cancel the license.
g) A mobile phone will be provided by the school in every bus so that in case of emergency driver or conductor could be contacted or they are able to contact school/police authorities.
h) It is the responsibility of the school that driver of the bus should not overtake any other four-wheeler on the road.
i) It is the responsibility of school management to provide training to children for embarking and de-embarking buses so that they are not injured in this process.

j) The school has the responsibility of parking the bus within the school premises while the students are using it.

k) If there is no space to park the bus inside the school premises, it should be parked in such a way so that other vehicles do not face any inconvenience.

l) The school should collect information about the conduct of the driver and the conductor of school bus and should keep record thereof.

7. For Parents

a) Parents are also equally responsible for the safety of children while sending them school.

b) It is the responsibility of the parents to know that the arrangements for transporting children to school and back to home are safe even if the said arrangement has been made by parents themselves.

c) If the bus driver, transporter or any other school employee violates any rule then the parents should immediately inform the school or state officials.

d) Parents must participate in the Parents meeting and should speak openly about children's safety.

e) Parents should not use vehicles that do not have a valid license or permit to carry the children.

f) The safety of children is a delicate matter and parents should be alert about it.

g) The above guidelines have been issued by the Central Board of Secondary Education after the orders of the Supreme Court. It is the responsibility of the school to accept them and it is the guardian's responsibility to know whether the schools adhere to these guidelines.

PARENTS THEMSELVES VIOLATE THE LAW

It is unfortunate that there is no rule related to school cabs in Delhi. In 2007, a policy was made to use private vehicles as a school vehicle but no one is following it. Most parents will not even know that there is any such policy or rules, nor do they have time to know about it.

Nowadays, schools are no more considered as a temple of education but only a money making shops. Therefore, the schools do not send their buses to such areas where they do not expect any profit. Parents of children living in these areas have to make their own arrangements to send their children to schools in privately owned vehicles under compulsion. Unaware of concerned rules parents engage any private vehicle for this purpose. In spite of knowing the danger of engaging private and unauthorized vehicle parents are helpless to make use of them having no other alternative arrangement.

- The capacity of the van is for eight children but are loaded 25 like sacks. Some children go to school sitting on a most dangerous CNG cylinder According to the rules no more than 12 children are allowed in an eight-seater van. Moreover these vans do not have permits nor do the permission from the transport department to use their vehicle for school duty. All these facts are known to parents very well but they close their eyes and keep mum. They wake up to the situation only after some accident happens with children traveling in private unauthorized vehicles.

There are some rules prescribed for school vans, but parents defy these rules for engaging vehicles with private registration numbers as school vans. They least bother to care for the rules. Their attitude is to face the music as and when it happens.

- School vans should not be more than ten years old but parents pay money for the vans which need to be sold to a scrap dealer and invite the dangers themselves.
- The owners of private school vans take the contract for ferrying children in many schools at a time. Sometimes same vehicle owner takes contact for three schools. It does not appear to be possible commuting children to three schools in the given time. With the result, the school van is driven hazardously on very fast speed against the prescribed speed limit. Newspapers are full of information that many school children die due to rash and dangerous driving.

It hardly makes any difference for private school vans operators how many challans they have paid for using an unauthorized vehicle as school van without proper permission or without a valid license. It becomes a matter of astonishment when parents too are not worried about this situation dangerous for their children.

There are so many other examples that can be quoted in this regard but instead of counting the accidents if the parents get alert such miss-happenings with school going children can be avoided in future. For this purpose, parents should know the rules related to private school vans. The Delhi Government had drafted a policy in 2007 about the use of school vehicles. But this policy is still a draft and nobody cares to follow it. When the matter is related with the safety of children parents must acquire some knowledge about this redundant policy also which may add to their knowledge the basic rules about the use of private school vans.

It may please be noted that transport vehicles and transport staff are the main factors behind the sexual abuse of children.

CHILD ABUSE

What is Child Abuse?

No child can be sexually exploited by an unknown person. Children are abused mostly by persons known to the family'. As per government statistics, more than 30% of children are sexually abused by well-known persons only. All these known persons are very familiar and most trusted people primarily responsible for child abuses. It means there is always a danger of child abuse by those who are considered as faithful persons. Parents have to keep an eye on such people. Some of these may include:–

1. It can be a person who visits your home frequently and spends more time with your children.
2. Relatives or their grown-up children keep giving gifts to your kids.
3. A person who is looking for opportunities to spend time alone with children.
4. Someone who starts rubbing children every now and then starts hugging them kisses to show love, makes them sit on his lap or tries to touch in other ways.
5. The person who passes more time with the children than the people of his age.
6. Giving gifts to children without any occasion.

7. Playing with children for more and more time.
8. Accompanying children in the playground.
9. Taking photographs of children in different poses.
10. Giving his opinions about children.

The aforementioned examples show the acts of people who try to exploit children. It is also important to understand which type of tricks these people use to woo children. Parents need to understand the tricks adopted by the exploiters. Some of such tricks are mentioned below:–

1. Child exploiters first take children into their faith. They do this task very slowly, in such a way that neither the children nor the parents are able to find out when the child has been caught in his fascination. Children are fond of love, who loves them, children begin to obey them.

2. After gaining the faith of children, they start exercising rights over them pretending to be a well-wisher. Some of the people like bus/van driver, conductor, guard, peon, and sometimes teachers exercise their authority over children.

3. They start touching children on unwanted places on the pretext of friendship with them. They pretend as if it has happened unknowingly and not done intentionally. Gradually, the number of these activities start increasing. The child cannot understand what is going on with him/her.

4. Showing the obscene picture to children and then talking vulgar things with them is a trick which gradually affects children's mind. After some time the kids start thinking that pornography is not bad. After influencing children with their dirty thoughts they start abusing them.

5. It is a very popular trick to give children different kinds of temptations. By temptation, they take children to lonely and secret places and abuse them sexually.
6. These people make a lot of excuses to take children with them. Sometimes they pretend to be ill and some time on the pretext of illness of children they take them along and try to abuse them.
7. Often children studying in the same school exploit younger children.
8. Mixing drug into toffee or any other food item.
9. Creating relationships with children on the pretext of teaching children without tuition fees or helping them with their homework.
10. Threatening children is also a popular trick. They exploit children with different kind of threats.

The most important thing is that the parents themselves knowingly provide sensitive information about children to their abusers. This information can be misused.

Peer Pressure

After study, children feel best to play together with their friends and have fun. This is also true that children learn a lot from their friends. No doubt the first effect on children's lives is of their parents. But when children meet their friends outside the house, they are influenced by their habits also. Exchanging views with other children of their age at school or in the playground they start feeling in different ways.

Child experts believe that children's friends play a very important role in their overall development. How they are influenced by their friends depends on the types of their friends. As are their friends so shall become the children. Most of the children wish other children to be their alter ego. Some children want others to follow their footsteps; they wish them to behave, to think and to act as per their decisions. Innocent children very easily succumb to their pressure. If such friends are good they must be having good habits and good qualities. Otherwise wrong type of friendship may lead them to wrongdoings.

If someone asks a spoiled child how he learned to smoke cigarettes, if the second is asked how he learned to lie and the third one is asked how he learned to steal, the only answer would be from my friends. It is clear that children learn good habits in the company of good friends and bad habits in the company of bad friends. And this company is not confined to childhood; it lasts longer from childhood to youth.

According to a survey, only 40% of children have the impact of their parents, relatives or their brothers and sister whereas 60% of children are affected by the company of their friends. If their company is good they will learn good habits and if their company is with spoiled children they will learn bad habits. It is a known fact that bad habits are learned quickly and it takes a long time to learn good habits. Most parents feel their child is too small to understand. Once he grows up he will be able to understand what is good and what a bad habit is. This thinking of parents is their biggest mistake. The habits learned in childhood die hardly rather some bad habits may spoil their entire life.

First of all, parents need to know how children learn bad habits. There can be several reasons. Some of them can be follows:–

1. Background of Friends

It is known to all that children are happiest with their friends. When these friends form a group they forget all types of worries and start enjoying as a group. But nobody knows when this happy group would turn into a big problem. Thinking of all children in a group can never be the same. Some children belong to the poor family, some children belong to the wealthy family and some other children are of very wealthy families. The behavior and thoughts of every child are related to the traditions of the family which affects all the children. Children belonging to a wealthy or wealthier family continue to exert their influence on other children, especially on children belonging to poor families. Nobody cares for poor children even if they are more intelligent than rich children. In such a situation, the children of wealthy families suppress the feelings of intelligent poor children, disrespect them and make fun of them. When this process occurs again and again, these children become the victim of an inferiority complex. The burden of feeling inferior becomes a difficult proposition for such children which create a stress in their mind. In order to show their potential and to get rid of mental stress, they start using drugs. Rich children also start sporting them with the result the entire group of children gets addicted to drugs. Apart from this the affluent children are stubborn, aggressive and demanding by nature which also affects all the children of the group.

2. Misunderstandings

Some children learn wrong habits due to lack of knowledge. They do not know what is good or bad and just start doing because their other friends also do this.

3. Demonstrate Bravery

Children do not like others making a mockery of them. In place of being a matter of mockery in front of other children, they start doing something that they should not do.

4. Hiding Weakness

Children who feel weaker than other children have a strong desire that the group of friends should include them also in their group. For this reason, such children are ready to do the work that other children want them so that they can join the group. Even if that work is wrong.

5. Power Exposure

In simple words, when a powerful person puts pressure on a weak person on the basis of his strength or his status, it exhibits power. It is a matter of grief that even in schools children nowadays display their power over comparatively weak children due to their physical or financial position or due to the high status of their fathers. There is no need to have any big reason for such a power game. It can be displayed on very small and petty matters like the appearance of a child, poor child being more intelligent, and being praised by the teacher, teasing one another, abusing, crying or combating. Sometimes the children start fighting because of jealousness and hatred. They may also fight over discrimination, caste, religion or because of the different culture. A child of a rich family may discriminate against a poor child and an intelligent poor child may discriminate against the stupid child. This fight or quarrel is not only confined to abuse but also involves hurting each another. Nowadays, children of 10-12 years carry knives or other sharp weapons in their school bags. Even some children take pistols also with them hidden in their bags. There are daily news stories in newspapers that a child in a school has killed another child.

6. Groupism

Because of mutual differences, children of equanimity make their own group. Children of such groups are of similar thinking and thoughts. Still, there persists some difference of opinion among the children of the same group. Every child is different from each other. Therefore their behavior will also be different. Due to such difference, if any child of the group falls in a bad company of friends, he may spoil the entire group of children. In each group, one or the other child is thus found who influences other children with their bad habits. Slowly, the whole group becomes a victim of bad habits. Despite this, children prefer to live in their own group. Being in the group creates many problems. Every child wants that all members of the group do not ridicule him, but respect him. To make their place in the group, the children start thinking that whatever bad or good other children are doing, they should do the same. This is the thought that gets embossed in the mind of children. Another reason is that no child dares to go against their group. To go against the group, he needs to have courage, for which he has to choose one or two friends who will accompany him. But it is rare because most children like to walk with their group. Because of being in the group, children have to do all that willingly or unwillingly that the group leader decides. Some children avoid this pressure with the help of their self-force, but it has a bad effect on other children. Most parents do not have the knowledge of the school group of nowadays because this did not happen in their childhood. For this reason, parents cannot understand the impact of the group on the children.

BAD EFFECTS OF GROUPISM

Distance from Family

Children have their own life. They do not like much interference from teachers or their parents in their day to day life. They think the entire world is their enemy as nobody understands them except the friends of their group. In this situation, children are more likely to get under the pressure of their peer group. They think friends are their only well-wishers and they tend to make a distance from their parents, family members, and other relatives. This is largely due to peer pressure.

The Problem in Education

Children obey the advice of their group in place of their parents and teachers. They think what their companions are saying or doing is right and all others are wrong. Such thinking creates obstacles to their education. They want absolutely to be like the members of their group. In place of studies, the group becomes more important to them.

Lack of Self-Confidence

Friendship pressure can also be good and bad. The impact of the group may bring down the morale of a self-confident child. Peers, pals, and buddies – whatever names you may give them – friends are an important aspect of children's life. Most of the time, peer pressure on children forces them to change their attitude and values so as to conform to group norms. When the group forces them to believe there is no confidence in them, they start losing their self-confidence that adversely affects their future life.

Harmful Habits

A normal child knows well that smoking, eating betel leaf, drinking or using other types of intoxication is not a good thing, but to show himself to be great, excellent and brave in front of friends he starts using all this stuff. In order to stay in the group, children come under pressure from other children of the group and become a victim of bad and harmful habits.

Feeling Embarrassed

Children studying in an average good school come from different sections of society. Everyone's financial and social background is different. Financial background leads children to squabble and hostility. The children of poor families or middle-class-family cannot afford large chunk of pocket money, because of which they feel embarrassed and ashamed in comparison with rich children. They start to underestimate themselves and get annoyed at their parents. This situation creates a sense of hostility in children. The children who do not participate in any group do not get affected by such a situation.

Children can Harm Themselves

Sometimes children face too much pressure from their group which they are not able to cope with. With the result, they lose their nerves balance and severe their relations with friends and family members. In such a situation their life becomes very tense. God forbid under the state of acute tension some children may attempt to commit suicide.

GOOD EFFECTS OF GROUPISM

It does not mean that parents should put too mang restrictions on their children and avert joining a group of their friends for fear of learning bad habits. There are many benefits for joining the group of friends. Living together in a group, children also get to learn a lot of new things. It is not necessary they would learn only about bad habits in the group of their friends.

By staying in the group, children compare themselves with each other. In this process, children begin to think about their life by analyzing themselves. Watching other talented children in the group they may also learn and adopt their good skills. Children do not get much knowledge from their teachers or parents as they may get from their friends.

Being in a group gives children an environment outside the house in which the children learn something that cannot be learned in four walls of the house. They interact with different children with different temperaments. Children get an opportunity under the influence of the group or their circle to gather more and more information about other children. They come to know how other children live their life, how do they study, what they eat, what are their interests, what do they like or dislike etc. These are some of the fields from where children may pick up some good habits also.

If a group or circle of children is good, by the grace of God, it can have a positive effect on their life and personality. With the help of some children in the group, who are called close friends and who do not put any kind of pressure, but encourage them to do something good, children start learning good things.

Groupism can neither be stopped nor can children be prohibited from joining a group of their friends. Parents will have to think their children are growing up and they need some personal space and independence. It is necessary to stop them from evil deeds, but not with the force or coercion. They have to be handled with love and affection. Parents have to be very alert about the friends of their children. Company of good friends is a boon and bad company may spoil their life. It is, therefore, must for parents to keep an eye on the friends of their children.

KEEPING AN EYE ON THE FRIENDSHIP OF CHILDREN

First of all, parents will have to see who the friends of their children are and what are their habits. Parents must gather some important information about their friends. But it is not an easy task as children do not divulge their private information to anyone. To collect such information parents have to play a game. They may invite friends of their children at their home on any pretext like a celebration of birthday etc. This gathering would provide enough opportunity to identify the habits of different friends of your children in the course of discussion and talks with them.

You have invited your children's friends, and you start scolding your child. The result of scolding children in presence of their friends may be very serious both for children as well as for parents. Children would no more respect their parents. Rather would be more inclined to their friends. In order to woo their friends, they would start accepting and following their bad habits also. Sitting with friends of children, parents can discuss their daily routine. In this discussion, the parents can get a lot of information about friends' habits, their hobbies, their likes, and dislikes. Based on this information, the parents will be able to identify the good and bad friends of the children.

Nowadays TV, Smartphone, Tabs have become a common thing for children. How children use them. What messages are sent to friends, how do their friends send posts. All these things have to be monitored. It is common for children to see TV but most of the parents do not know what their children are watching. This information can be collected from the friends of children in the normal course of discussion while sitting with them celebrating the birthday.

In today's busy lifespan, both mother and father are very busy. Neither mother nor the father has any time to sit with their children. They seldom find time to talk to them. In such a situation, children start looking for a friend who would listen to them patiently. Their search may end with a person who is already in habit of lugging, of telling lie, hiding facts, assaulting, stealing. In the company of such bad person children may also get spoiled.

Children can be easily attracted towards wrongdoings. Children learn bad habits faster than good habits. They do not take much of time adopting bad habits from other friends. As a result, they can fall in the company of wrong friends. With an open eye, parents may protect their children.

BE FRIENDLY TO CHILDREN

Parents can be and should be good friends with their children. Children learn good moral values of life in the good friendship of their parents. Children are hungry for love. All they need is attention. They are attention seekers. If the parents do not take care of their children and do not listen to them frequently, it creates tension in their mind. They need some time from their parents to release tension. With tension in mind, they start doing something wrong deliberately to attract the attention of their parents. Their repeated wrong actions in due course become their habit. Parents need to be more careful in this regard.

Most of the parents hardly know the daily routine of their children. To get the information about what do your children do throughout the day, the parent will have to spare some time for them. The easiest way is to sit with them and talk with them at length, share their problems and try to know what is on their mind. Keep in mind while sitting with children and talking to them do not show your excessive love. More than required love also affects adversely.

Children are not able to distinguish between good and bad friends. It is the duty of a parent to provide detailed information to their children. Children try to adapt things of their liking; things which make them feel better. Similarly, children become victims of the bad company which may spoil their life. Parents have to be alert all the time to protect their children from falling into the bad company of spoiled children.

Every person whenever he does something wrong has to repent throughout his life. He considers himself to be guilty in his mind all the times but never wants to accept his guilt in presence of others.

A feeling of being wrong pricks him every now and then. He remains tense. Children too are not left untouched by this process. In the company of bad friends, if they happen to do something wrong, it creates tremendous pressure on their minds, a vital reason for stress and strain. If the stress of children is not removed in time, then there are far-reaching consequences. Therefore, parents should keep their children away from stress. There are some symptoms of stress in children and it is very important for parents to know them all. Some of such symptoms are given below.

- Complaining against friends over petty matters
- Continue fighting with friends
- Change of temperament every minute
- Not paying attention to studies
- Being out of mood every time
- Facing defeat from friends
- Pretending to be sick of Headache, Stomach Pain etc
- Being nervous over small matters

Childhood is a very delicate age. It is very easy to seduce abuse children at this age. Along with the school, the children also come in contact with the outside world and external things and people that have a great effect on them. Childhood is the age of development for children. Children need to be cautious about their consistency, friendship, and their activities. In order to protect the children, parents should take some remedies in advance:–

Parents must support their children in their daily routine. Most parents may not be able to do this because of business and leave the job to other people especially when children are alone. On such occasions, these people have a great influence on the children and children can learn wrong habits in their company. Parents should make a list of the friends and of other people who are directly connected with their children. Advise the children with love and with their consent to sever all relations with such people who incite them for doing wrong. Parents should not only be nice. They should appear nice also.

If the parents rely heavily on their children and think that their child will not learn bad habits by staying in the bad company then it will be a terrible mistake. It can never be possible to retain good habits despite being in the company of bad friends. It is true that association inevitably breeds affinity.

The Impact of Modern Lifestyle

Not long before there was a time when parents, especially fathers, used to keep some distance from their children to keep a discipline in the house. Naughty children used to keep silence and peace stopping all their mischief on the entry of their father in the house. They were afraid of father's anger and were scared of saying anything to him directly. It was conveyed through their mother. Nowadays most consultants advise to parents to be friendly with their children so that children feel the freedom of discussing every damn thing of their lives with them. And they interact.

Persistence of this distance is as good as the conversation between father and children remains within the prescribed limits. If children are forced to tell everything of their life to parents, they may cross the limit of lying. With the changing lifestyle and advancement of technology, children are also adopting such changes and are behaving accordingly. Because of modern lifestyle nowadays children are brought up on the basis of the articles published in magazines or programs telecasted on TV where parents are advised to be intimate friends of their children. But because of the modern lifestyle children have started entertaining themselves on Smartphone instead of listening to the folk stories from their grandparents or going to play in the playground with their friends. Seeing cartoons on Smartphone they have started behaving like the characters of cartoons. In the process, they have stopped caring for elders also.

Naresh Goyal is a very successful businessman. His only son Manish is studying in the very famous school in the city. Father is very rich and loves his son very much. He is also an intimate friend of his son willing to fulfill his every desire instantly. At the behest of the son, he bought a big car to go to school, bought a huge TV to watch cartoons; he bought him a Smartphone of the new age. In spite of being treated like a child of the royal family, he was not attentive to his study. He always brought poor result in school examinations. Once he was scolded by his mother for his poor performance in eighth grade. What happened next was horrible. Manish took hold of the leather shoe of his father and threw it on his mother in anger. A stubborn child was not able to bear the anguish of his mother only because he was the dear friend of his father not accustomed to such scolding. Manish had done such nefarious acts before also, but his actions were not taken seriously. When parents overlook the small mistakes of children they start committing bigger mistakes. Such mistakes of children require to be nipped in the bud. The real thing is that there is no time with parents to pay attention to the proper development of children. Side effects of modern lifestyle are being faced almost by each and every family. Parents are engaged in the rat race of adopting latest lifestyle spoiling the future of their children.

What do children, in fact, want from their parents? A little bit of love and some of their time. But nowadays parents do not have any time to spare for children. In contrast, the parents are busy minting more and more money. Day in and day out to provide a better future for their children.

The goal of the parent differs from that of children. Parents are awfully busy earning money. No time spare for other things. On the other hands, children are longing to get some time of parents. When children fail to get time from their parents they feel lonely. With no other alternative except to do what they like most. In such a situation they shirk from their studies, watch dirty sites on their tabs, making friendship with other adults. In the absence of parents, some children spend their time playing games on the computer or listening to songs on MP3. In the absence of parents, children start feeling a loof. The problem of feeling loneliness can be more serious. In addition to being depressed, they may have many more problems like:–

- Due to the feelings of loneliness children start losing their inner strength. They feel as if there is no one to love them, no one to like them and no one to care for them. In such a situation they start losing their courage also and feel as if they are worth nothing. Eventually they start loosing the confidence.
- The feelings of loneliness creates sadness. They feel marooned themselves from other children. Not to think of meeting &

talking with someone, they sever their relations with friends and remain suffocated in their inner self. This adversely affects their health. They lag behind in their studies also. With faith we can do a little, without it we can do nothing.
- A child living in loneliness starts losing his skills. He lags behind in school study besides losing interest in doing other works also. If the child keeps doing something new then the excitement increases. If he stops doing new things, his mental balance starts to wobble.

If this situation persists for a long time, the children begin to understand that the parents, friends and other people have rejected them and nobody cares for them. To attract the attention of others, children start doing such things which they should not do, such as breaking the household things, calling bad names, squabbling and beating, disrespecting elders. Even some children start smoking, taking drugs just for attracting the attention of others. They wish others to think of them.

It more often than not happens with children whose parents are very busy. Either they are working in high positions or are the owners of big business. Being rich they employ several servants to take care of their children. But children do not like to be in the company of servants. They desperately need the company of their parents. The duty of parents does not end with giving chocolates, toys, and pocket money. Children can neither confine themselves to watching TV for longer time nor can they play with their toys beyond certain limit. It is only the presence of their parents which can help them from the trouble of loneliness.

The parents who are busier usually have no time to spend with their children and listen to them. A child can express his heartfelt feelings freely to none other than his parents. When parents have no time children are bound to keep his feelings within his own heart. This creates frustration in their mind. Everyone knows pent-up frustration generates enmity and enmity generates hostility. A hostile child may either commit suicide or may kill someone else. Nowadays newspapers are full of reports of children of 14-15 years of age killing their schoolmate or some of their relative. If figures are collected it may not be possible to explain them all in a few pages. In today's environment, it is nothing else but the negligence of parents that children are getting more and more violent. Some children do not even hesitate to kill their own parents.

These days teachers in school are also upset by the violent attitude of children. Children do not tolerate even a little punishment and aggravate the situation to the harassment of teachers. This is more true with children whose parents are harsh by nature and give maximum punishment to children even for their negligible mistakes. Parents work hard to provide maximum facilities for their children but they have no time to share their grief, their problems, and their feelings. If the parents dutifully start spending some time with their children it may work wonders in their development.

MONEY OR CHILDREN

Parents think that their children are the happiest because they have provided them with all the facilities available in the world. They possess latest modern pieces of equipment like Smartphone, tablets, personal computers, new clothes and all types of games. Over and above they are given so much pocket money to fulfill all their additional desires. In addition to that, there are two tutors to help them with school studies, two servants to look after them; there is an air-conditioned large car to go to school. After having provided such a luxury life parents think their children need not wish for anything else. They think their children are happiest children of the world. It is apparent that such type of parents weigh the happiness of their children on the scales of money. They think everything is going to be good if you have enough money. For them money is everything. If you think for a while you may find that the wealthy people of the world have a lot of money but they do not have two minutes of time to talk to their children openly. They will earn millions of rupees in the amount of time they spend talking to children. Spending time with children means losing money. They forget that money can purchase only means of leisure and not the happiness, money can purchase goods not peace of mind, money can purchase good beds but not the good sleep, No one can purchase either good moral etiquettes or high standard of character for their children by any amount of money. Nobody else on the earth can create high moral values of life in children except their parents.

When both the parents are working the economic condition of the house gets strong. When the financial position is good parents get involved in unwanted activities breaking up all the restraints and rules. They lose valuable time in all these futile activities which they could have easily spared for their children. They very easily can count on fingers hundreds of reason for not being able to spare any time for their children Just as:–

- Sometimes we go to club for relaxation
- The party is organized at the weekend
- When both husband and wife are working they need some time for recreation
- To do a lot of work on the day of the holiday

- Children like to watch cartoons
- Children like to play games on the computer
- Children are happy with their friends
- The evening is study time for children

There are a lot of other excuses with parents for not being able to spare some time for their children but there is no need to explain everything. The main point is parents do not realize the bad effects of their unwanted activities on the lives of their children. Parents must know the benefits of spending time with children.

BENEFITS OF SPENDING TIME WITH CHILDREN

Education Benefits

Spending time with the children is not only for their mental and social development, but also has a long-term good impact on their studies. Children, whose parents spend their time with children, are more intelligent and they have more confidence in themselves. The biggest benefit of living with children is that their parents can keep an eye on their daily routine and can overcome their weaknesses in time. As a result, children can perform well in their school exams.

Mental Stress

Some children are co-erced to live alone under compelling circumstances. Their parents remain out of the home all the day. They go out of the home before the children wake up from their sleep. Children go to school and come back, finish their homework, play in the evening. Parents do not return home even after children have taken dinner and are going to sleep at night. The mental stress of such children seems to be more than the other children. As per some experts, there is a deep relation between closeness of parents with children and personality development of children. The more the relationship will be, the child will not only be more intelligent but he will be full of self-esteem, moderate and obedient.

Attachment with Home

It is a fact as long as parents spend their time with the children; children dare not doing anything wrong. The purpose of spending time together is not to sit up together or to walk together. The real benefit of living together is by talking to children. Talking to children means talking about children and parents should not go on telling their own stories. They should listen to the heart of children. Listening to children is an art. It requires a lot of patience. If the parents patiently talk to children, the children will feel like having more attachment with home.

It has been observed that those children often become addicted to drugs whose parents do not spend enough time with them. Once addicted it becomes very difficult to quit this habit. It will not be sufficient for parents to say that there is no time to spend with the children. Parents can keep talking to children while watching TV while eating food, while shopping or driving. It creates a sense of attachment for the home in the mind of children. An attachment is also a kind of addiction. The children who are attached to their parents and home need not any other type of addiction.

Beware of Dangerous Habits

If children do not have an attachment to the house or with the parents, then the consequences can be very scary. Experts believe that children who are not attached to their parents can be involved in anti-social and criminal activities. They may get addicted to tobacco and alcohols etc., apart from this, such children begin to commit a number of other crimes, which not only adversely affect, but the goodwill of the parents can be on stake.

On the contrary, if children have an attachment to their parents, they feel someone is there to love them and a feeling of being important is developed in them. In this situation, they start obeying every order of their parents thinking them to be their ideal persons. The parents also learn about the attributes and qualities of their children which help them to guide their children to overcome their problems and weaknesses. In this environment children also gladly tell all their heartfelt feelings to their parents. When there is nothing hidden between children and parents, the attachment becomes more intense.

Stop Deciding the Future of Children

Most parents are licensed to decide the future of their children. They do not care what their children want to do. The parents simply impose their wishes on them. Some persons wish their son to be a doctor, other persons want to see them as an Engineer and many others may like to see them as big a businessmen. It is the choice of parents not the decisions of children. All of them want to impose their desires on their children. They get out of bounds if children show their interest in some other field. No one tries to listen to children. They just keep on forcing them to agree to what parents want. From this very point, the ideological difference between children and their parents start emerging. The child is inclined to a field of his interest but parents force him to the field of their choice. The difference in opinion on both sides widens and a stressful situation is created. Now parents having no other option use their authority and force children to agree to what they want. With the result the entire atmosphere becomes tense and children also get stressed. What is required here for parents is to understand the basic interest of children? The parents should freely discuss the matter with open mind and provide alternate options to them. Some options can be easy and some other options can be difficult. Sometimes the middle path can also be adopted. Psychologists believe that the parents should not use force with children, any forceful action may adversely affect and results can be bad. This may also create mental stress in the mind of children.

Become an Icon of Children

The main reason for the mental stress of children is the sense of insecurity. When children feel insecure their mental balance gets disturbed. The parent should present themselves as an ideal who can protect them in all conditions. When a child starts feeling that his family is strong and capable of protecting him, not only his self-confidence will grow, but he will also consider himself to be very strong. All this can be made possible only when the children's are attached to their parents and their families is strong. The relation of children's mental stress depends largely on how much their attachment to their parents is and how much their parents are concerned about their feelings. If there is a lack of attachment and parents are in habit of scolding them every time then children will surely become a victim of mental stress. The love and affection is reciprocal. It flows from higher level to lower level. Very much liquids.

Moral /Ethical Education

Someone has rightly said,

> *"If you can dream it, you can make it so. To educate a child in mind and not in morals is to educate a menace to society. Nowadays it seems that moral education is no longer considered necessary. Attention is wholly centered on intelligence, while the heart life is ignored."*

There was a time when children were taught the lessons of moral ethics in school. The book of every class had a biography of a great man who, after sacrificing his personal interests and all the comforts, had devoted his life to the welfare of the society. Now those good old days have gone when grandparents provided examples high moral values, good etiquette and high standard of character sacrificing their all comforts, self-interest, and amenities of life. Nowadays, politicians of criminal activity are becoming the ideal for children. Children are getting the education just to learn all good or bad lessons which suit their self-interest even if such learning is harmful to other people. Today, no one has the time to teach moral education or good values to children. Teachers think in terms of marks and ranks of student. They give importance to bookish knowledge only. And parents think that their children should grow up to earn more and more money. Children get misguided in such a situation.

Great industrialist Ratan Tata once said,

> *"Don't make your child Educated, make him a good human being."*

In the society, every person is identified for two reasons, his Ethics and his Education. If a highly educated person is characterless, his education cannot give him any respect in the society. If a person is less educated but is a man of high integrity with human values, the society respects him out of the way. Good human values are the essence of life. Ethic have always made the person happy. Those who lack moral ethics have to repent in life. Go to any old age home, children of most elderly people living there are doctors, engineers, industrialists or rich people. You will not find any single old person living in old age home whose children are uneducated or poor. The children of people living in old age homes are well placed and earning large chunk of money but they do not have space for their old aged sick parents in their home. It is an everyday story in newspapers about children who force their helpless parents to go and live out of the house. Some of the children even kill their parents to grab their property. The root cause of this all is the lack of good human values in children which parents have failed to part with.

If the parents can give some worth to their children then it is nothing else but good moral values. With good moral values, children learn to respect other people, they become companion of others in time of grief and happiness. They learn to feel a sense of belongingness. With the sense of belongingness, a sense of self-importance also develops in their mind. A cultured child always respects his parents, obeys their every command, living in grief they try to provide happiness to them. There is no need for any training to learn good rituals or human values in any university.

Good moral values are inherited by children from their parents. If the parents are cultured then their children will also become cultured. With good moral values, not only the future of children will be bright but it would rather enhance the reputation of their parents as well. Unfortunately, in our modern way of life, our values, character, and ethics are continuously diminishing. The life of the entire society has become very busy and is running at such a fast pace that neither teachers nor parents have time to teach good moral values to children. As a result, children's conducts are getting worse nowadays. In the tender age when children were expected to be busy in their study or in sports, it has become common for them to speak lie, to tease, to smoke, to steal, even to commit the heinous crimes like rape. Skipping classes and watching vulgar moves is now a common thing for them.

When children are involved in criminal activities, neither parents nor teachers have any time to teach them basic ethics of life. Children have no manners to use simple words like Namaste, thank you or sorry. Little do they know that courtesy costs nothing. At times it pays. They do not even regret their wrongdoing. They think what we are doing is fine. As a result, criminal tendencies in children are increasing day by day. This tendency isolates them from their parents as well as from the society. When the isolation in relationships increases children start behaving arbitrarily. See some examples:–

Violence in School

Every now and then newspapers are reporting incidents of violence in schools. If such violence is restricted to just hand fighting, squabbling, wrangling or calling bad names, it can be tolerated.

Children do fight with each other. So far so good. The most serious is now children take to arms in their schools. Many cases have been reported where senior children kill small children in schools.

Sullied and Dirty Thoughts

Due to the lack of moral values, the relationship of children is cut off from the family. Neither they respect elders nor do they care for them. Writing dirty and filthy things in toilets, addiction to pornography is a common thing for them. All these shameless and dirty ideas are polluting their mind. All these habits show that neither children have self-respect nor do they know as to how to respect others.

Common Manners

The general meaning of manners is the noble conduct with good behavior. But what is the behavior? We are known only by our behavior in society. Our behavior determines how society views us. Society recognizes us as a good person by our good behavior and vice versa. It means the behavior is what we do within the frame rules of the society. In other words, our behavior or conduct must be according to the rules and practices as prevalent in our society. These rules and practices of the society impose certain restrictions also. But in the modern lifestyle, most people do not like being in any kind of restrictions. Modern person is the one who does not accept any type of control or restrictions. Independent life has become the definition of modernity. The main mantra of a free life for them is "I am paramount", whatever I do is right. Such people also claim their wrongdoings as their right actions.

Modern persons do not care for other people's feelings, thoughts, sufferings, respect, and emotions. Drinking, smoking, not respecting elders, late sleeping, late waking, fast car driving, insulting others, discarding poor people, dirty and filthy actions. All these are justified by them with one and the same logic. That it is me, "This is my life, I am the owner, I will do whatever I want". They have nothing to do with what is morality and what are the manners. They even do not care about the law of the land.

If parents are having such a modern lifestyle, what will their children learn from them? Ethics play a big role in the upbringing of children. In the society wherever or whenever we meet other persons, we need to observe some ethics.

There is no limit to follow the norms of etiquette, ethics, and courtesy. In every walk of life, it is necessary to have the lowest etiquette in every field. For teachers in school, parents and elders at home, friends, neighbors for every one we have to show some courtesy. Even courtesy of eating food, manners of attending ceremonies, manners of speaking, and courtesy for guests, courtesy of meeting each other. There is no limit to observe the norms of courtesy, good manners, and etiquette. Courtesy means showing of politeness in one's attitude and behavior towards others according to time and place. Through manners, there is a glimpse of the inner civilization of the person, respect for others, aptitude of serving and the human values inherited from the parents. No one loses dignity by observing good manners, rather his prestige increases in society. When children display good manners, society not only appreciates those children but also praises their parents. The children who do not have courtesy in their behavior people do not curse them but their parents.

In short, it is the obligation of parents to teach their children good manners. At first, the parents used to worry more about their daughters but now the time has come when they get worried about their sons also. Teenage is a delicate age and requires special attention of parents because this is the age when children do not recognize what is wrong and what is right for them. In this age, children may fall prey to wrong activities. Serious mistakes of teenage children can be a cause of great problems for their parents. Hence parents of adolescents must take care of the following things:–

1. **Self-Respect:** If children respect others, especially elders, they will also get respect. Not only they would be praised but people would also admire their parents. This will strengthen the children's self-esteem and the children will begin to appreciate themselves. This will not only increase the confidence in them but they will also be happy. By adopting a positive attitude, the mental health of the children would improve. The children who are good at the rituals can handle difficult situation easily.

2. **Respecting Others:** Every day we meet a number of persons and ask well being of each other. In India, people greet even unknown persons. People do not just judge us from how educated we are, which school we attended and what is our status in the society. Neither they ask for our caste. We get respect from other people by virtue of our conduct. People respect us for our behavior, how we behave with them, how we talk with them, how we treat unknown persons, whether we extend any helping hand to needy with respect. In order to get respect from others, we have to first pay respect to them.

3. **Manners are Learned by Small Tasks:** The life of small kid of a poor lady who worked as a domestic help in the houses of rich people was saved only because of the good manners of that little child. This was the only child of a poor and illiterate mother who used to respect all elders of the society by saying Namaste to them. The trait was learned by him from his mother. While the children of educated people living in the same society did not pay any respect to anybody in their vanity. His life was saved because of his good manners. This rule applies to other children also.

   It is necessary to have good relations in society. This is possible only when we respect the feelings of others. When children hurt the feelings of their friends or other people or treat them rudely, people boycott such children. They do not want to have any relationship with them. Due to the boycott of friends, a line of strain is drawn in the mind of children that has its own bad effects. The children who pay respect to others and care for their emotions live a happy and healthy life.

4. **Popularity:** Children, who are kind to their classmates, express their sympathy; express their gratitude are liked by one and all. By paying respect to classmates, children's friendship is intensified. Children with good moral values are respected by all and they become popular among masses. People praise them everywhere even in their absence.

5. **Different Identity:** Children who are cultured acquire a distinct identity. To participate in any competition, to be a part of any school function, to organize a social event, everywhere teachers, school management, people of the society

provide more opportunities to the cultured children than other children. A separate identity increases self-confidence in children.

6. **Sportsmanship:** (The spirit of cooperation): Playing is the first hobby of every child. But, it has however, been seen that most children play only with the spirit of victory, even if they have to be dishonest to win the game by cheating. Winning a game by cheating and breaking the rules of the game can't be termed a victory. The children winning the games by cheating cannot feel happy in their heart. The parents, therefore, must encourage children to play honestly and according to the rules of the game without cheating. It is the matter of great pleasure to play a game with the spirit of the game where there is no importance of victory or defeat. It must be explained to children whether they win or lose but they in no circumstances should adopt unethical manners and cheating just to win the game. In case of losing the game, they must be encouraged to improve their skill by providing them examples of well-known players for doing more practice to be able to win the games honestly. The child who keeps on practicing is finally the winner.

7. **Parent's Behavior:** Most children do what they see while doing their parents. Whether there is a school, a house, a party or a function, children everywhere behave as they see their parents doing. Therefore, it is necessary that every parent should always behave well in front of the children so that their children can learn good values.

8. **Importance of Good Manners:** Good values are of universal importance. The good human values that children learn in their childhood become their lifelong assets. While good

morals can prove to be a boon for children; bad rituals can ruin their life. It is up to the parents how they wish to shape up the future of their children.

9. **The Main Mantra of Good Manners:** Good manners are not obtained by any degree of college. Every parent wants his child to take up higher studies. Giving higher education to children is their obligation, but it is more important to give children ethical education. No school or university is required for ethical education. The best school of ethics is at home. Good human values come not from big performances but from small habits.

10. **Kind Nature**: A kind-hearted person is like a God. The person who is kind at heart and has compassion for others is respected by all.

Tell children to be kind and considerate.

11. **Humility**: A humble child pleases everyone and wins over their hearts. Talking politely, not touching others' objects without permission, using words like sorry, thank you, pardon me are some qualities of humble children. Likewise, there are many other things that make them humble. Humility gives an opportunity to learn a lot from others. The more humble a person is, the more he can learn from others. With continued learning one can get immense success in life. Therefore, tell children to be humble.

12. **Accepting Responsibility**: Responsibility is required for every work in life. The bigger the task, the greater is the responsibility. By assigning small jobs in childhood Children

learn to take responsibility. The habit of accepting responsibilities is a key to success in life.

Tell children to be responsible.

13. **Importance of Discipline**: The definitions of discipline can be many, but in short, it is the greatest discipline to keep yourself under control. Discipline is the basic mantra of life. The disciplined person always leads to success and gets the appreciation of others. But children do not obey every discipline. The main reason is parents are not disciplined. We can understand that a man cannot live a disciplined life all the times but he can always act like a disciplined person in front of children. Small acts of parents have a great effect on children's minds. Therefore, even a little indiscipline of the parents can influence the mind of children

TELL THE CHILD TO BE DISCIPLINED

Every parent should understand the importance of good values of discipline, only then they will be able to focus on the need to learn good values for their children. Due to the lack of good values and discipline, the future life of children can jeopardize, rather they can learn bad manners as mentioned below:–

1. Disobeying parents. Being stubborn they persuade parents to accept unwanted demands.
2. Children can become selfish, harass others and become the mastermind of serious mischief.
3. Weak in study and copying in examinations.
4. The behavior of children can be negative.

5. They lose control over their works
6. They always remain sad and unhappy.
7. Children lack social qualities.
8. They cannot make friends with children with good manners.
9. There is a lack of kindness, sympathy, patience.
10. Begin criminal activities.

On the contrary, the children whose parents teach them to be disciplined and cultured can have the following qualities:–

1. Disciplined children can control themselves and they have more self-confidence.
2. Children begin to understand the responsibility of school and home.
3. Understanding their responsibilities, they do not do the wrong thing.
4. They not only help others but know how to behave.
5. Their thinking is positive.
6. They remain focused and can concentrate well on their study and other works.
7. Children are adventurous, can compete with difficult situations.
8. Cultural and disciplined children are more efficient than others.
9. They are obedient and respect elders.
10. They have a sense of humility for which they are liked by others.

Remember, good morals attract good morals and bad habits attract bad habits. Just as a rotten fruit destroys all the fruit, a bad habit ends up all good qualities. The old saying is that a filthy fish makes the whole pond dirty. Ethics can change but the man does not change. You might not have seen such a person in any country that is not hungry for praise. Appreciation is liked by everyone, but there are very few people willing to accept the good manners, ethics, and etiquette.

Always remember that the parents are the first ideal of the children and all children imitate their parents. Though parents cannot remain bound in the rules all the time, even then, they must follow as much as possible, good rules in front of children. Mainly keep the following things in mind:

- Honesty
- Hard work
- Speaking truth and sweet
- No confrontation in presence of kids
- Being kind and helpful to others
- Be patient and show determination
- Living in discipline and Eating Healthy

Technology

Once Albert Einstein had said,

"I fear the day that technology will surpass our human interaction. The world would have a generation of Idiots."

Nowadays, children are being brought up in such an environment where everyone is awfully engaged with new technology and the internet. In this race, children are not exception. They are also using the internet, computer, Smartphone, tablets, e-readers' to the maximum possible extent. A variety of different types of digital screens can be seen all around and everywhere. Need not to go anywhere else; the parents in every house are themselves spending their most of the time with these gadgets. Children as they come from primary to middle school, they become proficient in new technology. They become so skilled that they leave behind their parents in the field of technology. Some may start misusing it.

There is no doubt that technology has made life easier. Children can benefit from the information available on the Internet for education, get educational information from different types of apps and tools. They can consult their friends and teachers about studies. Technology provides many other types of facilities also like:–

BENEFITS OF TECHNOLOGY

1. **Systematic Studies:** Studies can be done smoothly by technology. Through technology, children are motivated to study not only with the help of different types of educational applications, but they are motivated to study in a systematic manner. They also enjoy educational Apps because these Apps are prepared in such a way that the children feel no difficulty.

2. **Information Available at Doorsteps:** Children do not need to go anywhere to gather education-related information. Sitting at home they can get any type of information they want, with great ease.

3. **The Convenience of Dialogue:** Technologies facilitate communication in children. They can talk whenever they want. This is also the best way for parents to stay in touch with children

4. **Mobility:** Smaller technologies like Smartphones provide mobility. Teachers and parents including children can take them along anywhere. Rather they can stay in contact with

each other. The classroom is now no more necessary for studies, children can study anywhere and anytime with the help of these Apps.

5. **24x7 Service:** This facility is available for twenty-four hours during the day and during the night. Against the fixed school timings. For the study on the internet, no timetable is required and children are free to start their study anywhere and anytime. The use of the Apps is quite convenient because of not having a fixed time. These apps are prepared according to the needs of children and they feel no difficulty in using them. Even small children can use them.

6. **Conservation of the Environment:** For traditional studies, we need to use pencils, papers, pens, copies, books etc., None of them is required in the study based on the applications. All necessary notes can be downloaded on the system. Thousands of trees have to be cut to make copies, books, and papers. Using modern technology all these trees can be saved which help in keeping the environment safe. The important thing is that with the help of Apps, children do their studies willingly and not forcefully.

7. **Entertainment:** Study is just a boring job for children. Most children do not like to study. But the children use Educational Apps available on the web with great passion. They enjoy making games of their book lessons and gladly complete their study. They even do not shirk of completing their homework.

8. **Support of Parents:** Apps related to education not only help children, but these apps are also very beneficial for parents and teachers. Teachers can use them in class and

parents at home. This will make the parent aware of which app is appropriate for their children. With the help of Apps, the parents can also monitor the activities of children. And it's very important.

9. **Contact Source:** Technology and Media acts as a contact source for children. Children get an opportunity to express their views, which not only increases their morale but builds self-confidence in them. When the child expresses his thoughts, he begins to understand the thoughts of his friends, parents, and others. By doing so, he broadens his thinking. He can take advantage of experiences of others.

10. **Nowadays**, technology is being used in schools for educating children. The benefit of using technology in schools is that children get acquainted with technology right in their childhood and they try to use it to the maximum extent for their studies.

HARMFUL EFFECTS OF TECHNOLOGY

A big book can be written in praise of technology. However some experts believe that technology is not as much beneficial for children as it is harmful. It cannot be denied that powerful tools and learning tools are easily available to children from different types of devices. Chat apps are also available for talking to friends. Worldwide information is available on the web. All sort of information can be collected in twinkle of eye. But children are still children, they do not know the right way of using technology. Their knowledge is half backed. Due to lack of complete information, technology can have a bad effect on the development of children. According to some researchers, the main harm of children is in development of their personality. According to these researchers, the following types of harms may occur:–

1. **Physical Strength**: It has been observed that nowadays children spend more time with the tools of technology. Because of this, their physical activities are becoming less and less. Physical exercise is necessary for proper development of the body, which can be possible only by running in the open and by playing sports. Sports and physical exercise increase the flow of blood in the body. The chemical flow increases in the nerves system of the brain and the brain of the children start working fast. Technology has reduced the physical activities at large. Children spend maximum time with the tools of technology and do not play and do not go out of the house. This can increase obesity on one hand and on the other hand, due to the excessive use of technology, physical exertion is minimized completely. When the human body stops doing physical exertion, then the desire to eat food declines. In the absence of nutritious food, human body faces many kinds of physical ailments. To avoid this problem, it is necessary to fix the time for the use of technology and the time of physical exercises. By doing physical work every part of the body is activated and it starts performing accordingly due to which much energy is generated. All the limbs begin to perform their function smoothly and properly. Suppose a child climbs on the tree. His whole body, brain and all the organs begin to work in coordination. All human organs start observing each moment of the child, not only the conscious but subconscious mind also starts functioning. All parts of body, legs, hands, fingers, eyes, arms, nose and ears all start working together. And what

does happen? Even in a dangerous and delicate situation, the child is able to maintain his physical balance. Is there any technology capable of awakening all the human senses at the same and the given time?

2. **Mental Impact:** Some experts believe that technology sharpens the brain. On the contrary, many specialists say that technology reduces children's personal capability. Nowadays, children do not use their brain in the same manner as people used to do before technology. Technology has narrowed their mind and children cannot develop any creative thinking. Rather, due to technology, children are not only subjected to stress in the school but outside school also. Due to the differentiation generated by technology in their lives, they become afflicted with other types of stress one after one. The technology creates more stress than relaxation. Every now and then messages are received and children keep on reading them instantly. Most messages are full of stress creating unnecessary tension in the mind of children. More often than not, messages are unwanted. But they vest in sub-conscious brain. They keep pricking. Perpetually and perennially.

3. **Personality Development:** As per inventors of technological devices, these are helpful in schools for the education of children. But child experts believe that with the help of technology, children can play educational games but they do not agree that these games or apps are actually helpful in the education of children. According to them such educational games or apps are just pieces of show. In fact, such devices are obstacles in the development of children. Children cannot make their independent decisions by using

educational devices. Nor can they create their own independent thoughts. Most importantly, the parents also think that the educational tools will increase the knowledge of children and the children will learn new things. The reality is that children learn something from the real living experiences in life rather than from the devices. Children learn from what they see. If the parents themselves do not make any effort and keep the children independent of the tools, then how would they learn anything? Children follow their parents. They will do what their parents are doing. When children see their parents using latest equipments, they also fall in the line. In this process what happens is that children do not develop as children, they start behaving as adults. Parents are ideal for children and they should behave like ideal human beings. Nowadays every child has a Smartphone for spending most of his time. As a result, the ability of reading and learning in children reduces and they also lose their time in googling their phones.

4. **Lack of Self-study:** Children use technology for their entertainment as well as for school work. Without the help of the U-Tube, the children cannot even do their own homework. To get any information they start clicking their phones. After getting desired information they copy it right there. The practice of writing by hand and holding the book in hand is decreasing. Mathematics calculations are now done by children either on calculators or on some other device for which they do not need to use their brain. Slowly it becomes their habit and later they find it difficult to solve small questions without the help of technology.

Most of the children are dependent on the internet for their small tasks. Although this helps the children, it is not necessary that they may get the right type of information from the net. Anyone can post anything on the net and the information received on some posts may be wrong. Children do not know which information is correct and which is wrong. Wrong information can have adverse effects on their studies.

5. **Dangers and Deceptions:** The benefits of social media are numerous. Children can get the desired information any time and about anything: They can talk to their teachers and friends, consult them and solve their problem, but on some social media, some deceptive people are also engaged in enticing children. The people of perverted and corrupt minds are also active in abundance on the social media; they may be a risk for children. By creating Fake Account, these people may become friends of children and later entice them for wrong activities.

6. **Inappropriate Contents:** Some useful information available on the net can help children in many fields of their activities. But at the same time, children also receive such material on the net which is not suitable for them. While using the net for studies, many harmful contents may appear on the screen to influence their mind. You must know that nothing on social media is prohibited or censored. Children can also see violent videos, videos of sex, videos of drugs and the videos teaching them how to commit a crime successfully. Thereby leaving menacing effect.

Such type of information can certainly have bad effect on children. Along with this, the children like to watch their favorite film heroes or sportsmen. By looking at them, the children can also try to copy their clothes, methods of living. By doing so, children start living in a hypothetical world away from real life and start fictitious hopes that can lead them to the world of crime.

7. **Disturbance in Daily Routine**: Remaining 24 hours busy with a technical device can disturb the daily routine of children. Children stay awake overnight using it. Because of this children do not get complete sleep their sleeping habit becomes irregular. Even if they want to sleep on time they fail to make. Staying awake overnight not only affects their health but it causes memory loss also. Children under the age of 12 may have serious problems with the use of technology more than required.

Parents should not allow excessive use of technology to small kids. Excessive use of technology in this age is not only a hindrance to the development of children but also causes physical harm to them.

DANGEROUS AND CRITICAL PROBLEMS

1. Radiation

The most dangerous for children is the radiation emission. First, you have to understand what radiation is. Radiation is an energy which spreads in the atmosphere in the form of waves or molecules through air, noise, water, substances, insect disinfectants etc. Radiation is emitted in two ways. One form of radiation is pure in which there is no weight, only beating or vibrations are there and it is called electromagnetic radiation. This type of radiation flows in the form of electrical or magnetic energy such as radio waves, microwaves, x-rays, cosmic rays etc. The second type of radiation is called molecule radiation; it has weight and size also. These are very subtle fast moving molecules known as alpha, beta, and neutron. It is a lesser-known form of radiation. The above information about radiation has been given just to explain it in simple terms, it should not be considered scientific or authoritative. The purpose of this is to explain to parents what the radiation is.

About the first type of radiation which emanates from cell phones, WHO had considered it to be a cause of cancer for children and declared it as a threat of the category of 2B. Based on the afterward research work in this field WHO described it to be a threat of higher grade and categorized it as 2A which is the more dangerous cause of cancer for children. You will be surprised to know that the radiation of this type of radio frequency / electromagnetic frequency is mostly generated from radio, television, microwave oven, cell phone, Wi-Fi. etc. In today's time, it is impossible to keep these devices away from children but they can be advised to use them at most minimum level.

Although the companies provide instructions for taking safeguards against the risk of radiation in their manual but nobody reads them. Even if some people read but they do not follow. I had, for example, read these instructions of a cell phone company and found written.

> *"To reduce exposure to RF energy, use a hands-free option, such as the built-in speakerphone, the supplied headphones, or other similar accessories. Carry iPhone at least 10 mm*

away from your body to ensure exposure levels remain at or below the as-tested (exposure-limit) levels."

Neither the children nor their parents pay any attention to these warnings. They keep their Smartphone in the pockets near their chest all the times. Please read carefully the opinions of the experts given below and try to advise children to avoid the effects of radiation emitting from cell phones:–

- Children are supposed to behave like children. But nowadays parents are also busy to look like techno savvy. Possessing of latest type of equipment has become a matter of fashion for them. Everyone is competing in the race of purchasing latest models of newly introduced devices.
- Cell phones and other wireless devices are harmful to the human body as they contain disruptive radiation of radio frequency.
- Some devices have electromagnetic waves which have a very bad effect on the brains of children because children's brains are more receptive to these waves in comparison to adults. With the effect of these waves, children may suffer from the dangerous disease of brain tumor and cancer.
- This increases mental stress in children.
- The nervous system is automated in the human body. More use of modern equipments by children can seriously damage their automated system. Nowadays, this disease is being found more in children. Its symptoms include a headache, dizziness, nausea, pressure on the brain, unconsciousness, pressure in the chest, irritability, weakness, and fatigue. Sometimes cardiovascular also becomes irregular.

- With the use of excessive and needless modern types of equipments, young children may also be subjected to insanity: In the initial stage, children start forgetting small things and gradually the disease begins to take on serious form. Experts call this condition by the name of Digital Dementia.

2. Digital Dementia

It is a term which first German Neuroscientist Manfred Spitzer had used in his book of the same name. This term was used for those who were in habit of using digital technology in abundance. Because of which they were losing their memory like a person who loses his memory because of serious head injury or suffering from some mental illness.

Children in habit of excessive use of digital technology also start losing their memory gradually and suffer from the disease of losing memory. The elder people still remember the names and telephone numbers of known people by heart but the children living in the existing environment do not remember any name or number as they depend on their digital instruments for this purpose. The excessive use of digital instruments by children adversely affects the development of their brain. To a large extent.

Should this not suffice, it continues to have other bad effects on the children. Effect of radio frequency reduces the ability of reproduction. DNA is harmed, which not only affects the health of the children, but they can also pass on generations to come.

It has a bad effect on the nerve system of our body that regulates our heart and maintains the balance of our body.

Children do not have the knowledge to save them from the effects of radio frequency, as such parents should keep the children away from such devices which have a high volume of radio frequency.

Nowadays, some schools have been using industry-level WiFi, which is more powerful than domestic WiFi. Its effect is not limited to classrooms only, but also of crossing the cement walls, the whole school, even in the open ground.

Keep in mind that radio frequency effects more to children who use items made of metal like stiffs, badges, nameplates or any other such objects made of metal.

The faster the technology is developing and the way new devices are coming into the market, it is impossible to calculate the number of devices that are harmful to children. In short, the main effect on children can have the following adverse effects:–

1. Intriguing Program

There are various types of programs that are liked by children in modern digital devices. Children want o see them again and again. It is the innate nature of human being that he feels to see or use a device again and which he likes most. Of course, many such programs may be good for children and beneficial also for them, but it cannot be denied that some programs may be even more harmful to them. The habit of watching most liked programs, again and again, is a type of addiction. The Researchers have named it as Reward Pathway. According to this theory, the most intriguing object is like being in a habit of intoxication. Children can also get used to intoxication by watching their most favored programs, again and again, that may lead to being in habit of actual intoxication. The parents should take care of this with complete alertness.

2. Adverse Effects on the Power of Understanding

Every person has to do different types of activities in a given time and sometimes he is required to do a number of activities at a time. All through his mind keeps collecting information about such activities through communicating senses like nose, eyes, ears, mouth flavor, touch etc. This is a natural system. Elder persons do not feel any much trouble with this system. When children use technology equipment excessively, many different types of information are reported in their brain at the same time. In order to organize a lot of information at a time children's mind has to bear a lot of burden. As a result, it can adversely affect their power of understanding. Gradually children start losing memory of their daily activities and may need help from others at every step of their daily routine. They may forget even to distinguish between bad and good activities. They may stop feeling any type of sensation and may perhaps be not able to visualize the sense of acute pain, if they are suffering from.

3. Multitasking

The child wants to do a lot. And that too simultaneously at a given time. Technology has provided a new tool in the hands of children called Multitasking. Children think that they can do many tasks simultaneously at the same time with the help of their Smartphone or Tab. It is a great feeling but just to watch and to see. The question is whether or not it really is of any worth? According to specialists children are more at a loss rather than gain. Proportionally, the loses suffered by children are much more than that of elders.

For Example:

A child is trying to solve some of the math questions sitting at home. Simultaneously he is also watching a serial on his Smartphone. After about two hours, he comes to know that half of the math's questions he did are wrong. He also missed watching the major portion of favorite TV serial on his Smartphone. What now? He will have to solve all the questions again and will have to watch the missed portion of TV Serial again. It is just wastage of his precious time. It is clear from the above example that multitasking has a problem for children to focus on. Due to lack of attention, many other problems may arise. In an attempt to perform multi-tasks at a time children are spending their much of the time with digital equipments. In this process, they fails to keep the human touch with their parents or friends. In the absence of direct connection with people and being connected all the time with gadgets, they starts feeling loneliness. This can pose a risk of creating difficult conditions in the future.

Fact remains that doing one act at a given point of time not only the quality of the work is improved but it enhances the proficiency of children. By doing many tasks at a time either the work will remain incomplete or it will not be of satisfactory quality and may be faulty. It cannot be said whether or not multitasking enhances the skill of children but as per the opinion of specialists, it certainly has a bad effect on the mind of children. Children are not able to connect their mind with their actions. According to the child experts, when children do multitasking, in this process, they have to make many decisions instantly; they have to understand and have to act accordingly. It creates an unnecessary burden on their immature minds. It becomes a hindrance to the progress of children. According to the experts it causes following harms to children:

1. Children can commit more mistakes.
2. It creates unnecessary stress in their mind.
3. Their memory may diminish.
4. Children cannot do practical work.
5. Their direct contact with family and friends diminishes.
6. Children may not be able to perform any creative work.
7. Cannot communicate effectively with others.

If children have to be protected from these evils, then it has to be kept in mind that children should avoid multitasking. Here also the obligation comes only with the parents.

4. Dangers of Children's Health

Nowadays, the trend of information and communication technology is increasing in more and more schools, where children are always in contact with some electronic device. To make this communication more convenient, children are also encouraged to use WiFi and children are also using it. The use of such devices must be kept to the level where the risk of radiation is minimum. Lest, it may effect on their health. A lot of discussion has taken place in this regard, but no suggestion is forthcoming with this problem.

In childhood brain is not fully developed. The tissues and muscles of the brain of children are also weak. Moreover the brains of children are small and immature compared to adults. Consequently, the children's muscles are quickly affected by radiation and, they are more at risk of radiation in comparison to adults.

If compared with adult's children are more affected than the 5 Kg of their body weight by the outer electromagnetic field. A 6-year-old child consumes 60% more energy than adults. In Bone Marrow, its effects can be nine times in children compared to adults. Children's brain membranes are thin and the effects of radiation can give them persistent life-threatening.

What happens is that mobile phones or other microwave generating devices affect the nerves of children's brains (electrical activity of the brain). These nerves send information from the brain to different organs of the body through the nerve cells. The function of receiving and sending information is centered in the brain. While applying cordless devices, electrical waves rising from these devices affect the waves flowing through the brain of the children. Therefore, the connection between children's thinking and their actions decreases or gets disturbed. Whether it has any immediate effect or not, but long-term effects can be very high. In scientific research, it has been found that due to the use of these instruments for a long time, brain cell can be eliminated and as a result, there can be loss of memory of children and they may feel difficulty in learning something new and even they may feel difficulty in performing daily routine tasks and taking decision related to such tasks. In children, the ability to fight disease can be eliminated; affecting the DNA, obstruction of the natural development of the brain, and their behavior and hormones can also be affected. Not only this, there are more online threats for children.

7

Online Threats for Children

Most of the people have one and the same opinion that the digital technology is very helpful in the development and education of children. Today every child has a Smartphone in hand and the child also uses it a lot. But the more children use the information and communication technology, the more they put themselves in many on-line hazards.

Newspapers are filled with news of children becoming victims of cybercrime. And these crimes are increasing day by day. Every child can come in the grip of such crimes anytime. The culprits induce children for crimes. Many of them even start committing crimes after watching them. Digital technology teaches new ideas of crimes. The style of crimes used earlier is the same but online crimes are more serious in nature. The offenders first attract children through the online system and lure them away to make real connections with them. Once a personal connection is established they involve them in activities of criminal nature.

Below is described how online crimes are committed with children:–

a) **Cyber Bullying**

This threat is given to children through digital devices such as cell phones, computers, and tablets. The way to bully can be SMS, written (text) or different types of apps. This threat is given in such a way where children can see and read them easily. This threat involves harmful things, defamatory things, false information, dirty talks, private and secret information, or such information that children are afraid of. The threat is given either you accept doing what we want or your private information will be made public. Such activities are done by the people of criminal aptitude. They try to do everything possible to trap the children in their clutches. By such type of threats, they take emotional advantage of the feelings of children. They threat to defame their parents, insulting and boycotting them in their social circle. They mentally disturb the child to such an extent that the child is constrained to obey and becomes a victim of the criminals

Under fear, children report on-line threats neither to their parents nor teachers on-line threats to children can occur anywhere in social networks, video games or mobile phones. It can be sent to children at all times and everywhere and children cannot escape from it.

If the parents are cautious, it is not too late to pin point online threats. If there is a message on a child's phone, a tweet or a post on Facebook, where the child is threatened, be it obscene, be it personal information, filthy and obscene photos/videos, or videos that have been created to harm children, it should be presumed that a criminal is blackmailing the children. There can be following types of threats:–

- Dirty talks and filthy abuses.
- Dirty written messages or crappy gestures.
- Messages to scare bully or humiliate.
- To criticize, or spread rumors.
- Efforts to control and forcing to work on their lines.
- Messages of sexual abuse or lesbianism.
- Making false, insulting or derogatory calls.

If all this is happening with the children it can lead to various types of risks. They will lack self-confidence and self-esteem. Their feelings can be hurt. It will not be out of place to say that the security of children can also be a serious threat. Children may hide from their parents if they watch such sites which they should not see. They may be doing everything secretly. It is the parent's duty to sit with the children from time to time and talk to them and try to get to know their minds so that they can save them from cyber hazards during such situation.

b) Sexual Abuse of Children

Technology has made available to criminals accessible means of contact with anonymity. While these criminals cannot be identified, they can use these tools easily and conveniently when they want to. And worst is that such like criminals get away. Therefore, there is no fear in their mind of being identified or caught while committing the crime. This facility is available to them on the internet where there is no risk of being identified or being caught. This is possible if the crime is committed directly face to face in real life.

Nowadays, children use maximum devices. They have the facility to talk to people who otherwise are not permitted. Such conversations are kept secret from their parents. In such type of conversation, if the person on the other end is of criminal mentality, he may try to seduce children by his affectionate talks and offer some kind of covetousness. They mostly succeed in their attempt to win over the children. They gradually seduce children. They do not interact with children first, but show them sexual images and show how such images are formed. In the process of making images, they also give children the knowledge of having sex. They often hypnotize them by showing naked pictures of sexual activity that children are trapped in. They create so much excitement in the minds of children that they forget to distinguish what is bad and what is good for them. They start doing everything that the culprit wants them to do.

ACTUAL CHILD ABUSE

When children fall into the trap of criminals, they feel being captivated to accept their every decision. Criminals begin to exploit. Thereafter they start compelling children for sexual activity by pressurizing them or by covetousness. In exchange, they may offer attractive gifts like cash money, clothes, food, living facility, drugs, alcohol, cigarettes and most important love and affection.

Love and affection are most attractive for children. But in the love of criminal, there remain hidden desire of having sex. If for any reason children do not accept their offer; criminals use a very effective trick of creating fear in their minds. They create so much fear in the children's mind that children are forced to obey them in their every decision. When the children agree with greed or intimidation, then the offenders themselves first make sexual relations with them and then other people join. By making films, videos or SMS of children's sexual relations, they start blackmailing and exploiting them. They do not hesitate to take any action to trap the children whether they have to rape children, threaten them, scare them, beat them.

The purpose of the criminals is to earn money from child abuse. Nowadays, there are different apps available with criminals through which they can lure children for sex, recruit them, rape them, and then force them to have sexual relations. Experts believe that children around the world are being victimized for sexual abuse. This number is increasing day by day. It includes children from every class of society whether males or females.

Children usually go astray after seeing attractive and intriguing advertisements on various sites on the internet. In fact, such attractive advertisements are only given to woo children, especially those advertisements that lure children for friendship and take them on the path of disorientation. These ads have a captivating attraction. Due to this attraction children get caught in the clutches of an unknown vicious circle.

There is a case of a meritorious student, who is not only the best in studies, secures good marks and gets first place in every class. He seldom uses any computer, prefers to play outside the house in his spare time with friends. Seeing another friend playing the game on the computer, he not only started playing games on a computer but also enjoyed it. One day, his friend also taught him to chat on the computer. Slowly he started enjoying chatting and he started spending more time chatting. Now he spent more time on the computer and started exploring different sites. Once, he clicked on the Friendship advertisement on one site. The number of his online friends began to grow rapidly. Now he stopped to spend more time in his study and also he stopped going out to play with his friends. He was now busy doing something on the computer all the times. Both parents were employed, so there was no one at home to check. While browsing the site of Friendship, he found the site of the Escort service one day. He found as if has gone into a world like a heaven. All around there were beautiful girls full of glamour. He was lost in this fascinating and attractive world without knowing it was a porn site. Ultimately he was in a trap of pornography. Pertinent to say that his excessive use of technology ruined his life.

It is not an isolate case. It has now become the story of very mang houses. Most of the children in every house hide their activities from their parents and keep exploring such sites that may ruin their lives. It is absolutely essential that every parent monitor their children's computer usage. Prevent them from chatting with unknown people. If there is a need to chat with such strangers, children should be taught not to disclose their names, house address, family information. Password should not be disclosed at any cost. In no way.

To prevent children from pornography, experts have recommended certain measures of safeguards. Parents can block any site by using any of these measures. Nowadays all parents also use a computer and they are having such information as well. Those who do not know about this, they can adopt the simplest way written below:–

To block any site, go to the Internet Explorer by going to the Tools menu in the Internet Explorer and clicking in the Content tab. Then go to Content Adviser and click on the enable label. Now the Rating tab has to be opened, which has many options like language, nudity, sex, violence etc. Below there will be a slider. Now the limits of viewing them by choosing each one from language, nudity, sex, violence can be decided. If you choose sex then after setting the limits, the sexually-linked site cannot be seen on that computer. There are many other methods also but parents need to be alert and active all the times. There are a number of software available in the market that can block the objectionable sites. These can be used to protect the children.

The studies of some experts have shown that problems related to the internet among children are increasing day by day or the purpose of bravity. It is difficult to describe everything here but however there is a need to pay attention to some essential things. Nowadays children use so many devices that they are called Internet kids. When there is nothing to do they get the chance to explore the internet. Researchers believe that there are millions of web pages that lure children and children also come in their hoax. Most of pages are harmful to children. There are three main types of risks, mainly from Internet technology.

1. Subject Matter or Contents Related Risk:

These risks include inappropriate and illegal contents, harmful contents, harmful suggestions or advice, online hypnosis called cyber grooming, harassment, conversation, talk about illegal topics, problematic contents and unnecessary transmission of secret information. All topics can not be described in detail, however some of the main topics for parents' information which can be detrimental to children and which can online be used by children unknowingly are as follows:

- Children can watch videos where actual violence has been shown or children have been motivated to commit violence. Seeing such videos, children may be subjected to violence.
- There may be some sexually explicit contents. Most children are more affected by such type of contents.
- Some criminals prepare sexual material (photos) of children and then blackmail them.
- Contents that promote hatred based on gender, caste, religion, character.
- Contents that encourage children to commit violence or crime.

2. Personal Information and Safety Risk:

Collecting personal and confidential information from children, sharing this information with many people, unseen threats, malicious codes, and commercial spyware etc. are areas which are harmful to children. Maybe, most children are in habit to share information with people through online. It may be possible that some of their secret information is collected by harmful people. Children may also receive on-line information about malware, spyware or pornography along with the other information received by them.

The problem of Phishing can be the most serious. While searching online, criminals attempt to obtain secret information, personal or financial information from children by sending a fake mail or a fake message to children. The criminals can misuse the secret information obtained

Similarly, hackers use the Farming method to divert the contents of the people posted by them on the websites on some other site where they wish them to post. Through this method, hackers can influence many people at the same time and take them to a wrong or criminal site. If children accidentally reach this type of site then it becomes difficult to avoid criminals.

Children sometimes download some APPs on their phones or social networking pages. People who make APPS may receive information related to children that have no relation to the use of that APP. The information thus obtained in this manner is for the lone purpose of misuse. The criminals can also collect information from children by chatting with them like children. The only way to avoid these dangers is that parents should explain to their children that they should remain contacted online only with their known people, friends or relatives.

3. Money Related Risks:

These risks relate to advertisements of inappropriate goods for children, the sale of illegal items, spending excess money, identity theft, online fraud, rigging etc. In addition, there are many other online scams too. Money is taken from the children on the false pretext of their winning of a big reward. The task of selling dangerous drugs to children is also increasing nowadays The children can easily reach to advertisements which are exclusively meant for adult people The internet does not distinguish between children and adults.

Children have become so accustomed to technology that they keep using one or other device every now and then. They do not know what to post on the network and what not. The number of crimes related to children is revealed by the fact that most such crimes are due to the contents posted by children on the internet. The children can not foresee the potential danger and they post sensitive material out of excitement. Generally, children begin to use social networks, blogging platforms and other web applications at younger ages and post some information, messages, pictures. This may contain sensitive, information related to them or their family. Mistakingly they think that the information they have posted will be confined to their known people only. Some people in their lives may be like those who may later end their friendship or may turn an enemy for some reason. Such people can pass on such sensitive information to criminals.

CHILDREN'S OWN ACCOUNT AND DANGEROUS SITES

It has been seen that small children also open their accounts on social media and then fall in the company of wrong people. Some responsible parents understood this problem and started a discussion. Consequently, the Delhi High Court asked the Indian government why children under the age of 18 are allowed to open their account on social media. Similarly, UNICEF has also expressed concerns about the safety of children. Even after taking safety measures children find one or the other way to continue their online activities. It would, therefore, be better if the children are made to understand the online problems and they be advised to use it carefully, wisely and with caution. The children may sometimes unknowingly reach a site that can be very harmful to them such as Darknet. The Darknet is a site used for the criminal activities related to children. This site on the Internet cannot be traced through Google or other search engines, hence it is also known as underworld site. For this, criminals use a special type of software. It is very difficult to identify criminals. The information gathered here is hidden in many layers like an onion and on its destination; it reaches through the same layers. Once the notification or picture is posted, it cannot be erased or deleted. When the information reaches with the offenders, they choose their prey and then they start their criminal activities.

Video Games

There is no childhood without games. Children grow up by playing games and taking part in sports. Sports not only improve the health of the children but also develop their body and mind. A healthy body is a home to a healthy mind. Researchers believe that sports help in the all-round development of children. When there were no video games in the past, all the kids went out of the house and used to play different types of games. It was good not only for their physical health but also their mental development. They would befriend many other players.

With the advent of new technology, children have forgotten to go out of the house. Every now and then they play games on their Smartphone or computer within the house. Not only children, but other people in the family also like these games. Playing video games does not benefit as much as playing in the playground, but they have some advantages like:–

- Concentration: Video games teach children the art of concentrating hands, eyes and brain.
- Problem-solving, planning, instant decision-making and increasing logical strength.
- It is helpful to choose goals and to achieve them.
- Teaches to finish work in the time limit.
- When children win any of the games, their confidence increases.
- Stay in touch with friends and make new friends.
- The Memory and retention power of children increases.

To say it can have many more benefits, but it becomes a matter of concern when children start spending all their time playing video games. Playing video games for a longer period will also be a disease. In the new list of diseases released by the World Health Organization, video game addiction has been described as a mental illness. In place of their study or outdoor games children spend most of their time playing video games. Many serious problems arise like:

DEFICIENCY OF PHYSICAL AND MENTAL ABILITY

When children spend more than required time playing video games their desire to go out of the house for playing starts decreasing. They also stop participating in extra-curricular activities. By decreasing physical labor, neither the muscles develop properly nor does the brain. Children gradually fall behind in other works of life also.

1. Tension

There is no harm in playing video games for entertainment. For a short period of time. If the children play for longer periods, mental tension increases with the ups and downs in the game. If the mental stress exceeds one limit, the flow of blood stops moving towards the direction of the higher sensitive cells of the brain. The blood flow increases in those areas of the brain which are more sedative for life-saving. As a result, children start facing difficulty in performing others works. Most of the brain nerves of children are underdeveloped. Now that they have not developed fully children's brain is more vulnerable in comparison to adults. It is known to all that the stressed person gets disturbed soon and begins to do unwanted actions which can at times be dangerous.

2. Health Loss

Along with stress, other problems related to health also come up. In video games, children neither eat on time nor sleep on time. Apart from this, the children who watch more than two hours of television or video games instead of playing real games are surrounded by a lot of other obstacles, and they start having many types of physical disorders, including headaches, back pain, dizziness, and pain in eyes, in their wrists, hands, shoulders, and knees.

3. Sourness in Relationships

If children spend more time playing video games instead of real and face to face chatting with their family members or friends, relationships can be in trouble. Most of children do not disclose their time of playing video games to their parents and just pretend to be busy in some educational or other important task. On obstruction from parents, they start arguing with them. If there is such a situation, then the parent should be careful that the child is addicted to video games. It is not easy to get rid of any kind of addiction. And it is addiction to internet that keeps them alienated from real face to face interaction with their relatives etc. Much of the media coverage surrounding young people and online social networks has focused on the personal information teens make available on these networks. This has its own affects. More likely, negative. It is also possible that some unknown persons who play online games or handle some unknown websites may come to know a fact about children that they lie with parents about the time of playing their video games and do not tell the truth. The strangers are more likely to contact teens online than offline. Tricksters catch them and young.

4. Aggression and Violence in Children can arise

Children who play violent video games, especially those children who are addicted to video games, their behavior becomes violent too. Such children turn to violence instantly. No surprise if such children may act violently with their parents also. Experts believe that anti-social views begin to arise in the minds of children playing violent games. Parents also are a part of the society. Even if we do not talk about the society, because of their violent attitude such children may kill someone under the spell of violence. Killing animals becomes a game of entertainment for them.

5. Loss of Study

If a child is in habit of playing video games for more than much longer time he will certainly be lagging behind his studies. By playing till late at night, his mental and physical strength continues to diminish. He will neither able to concentrate on his studies nor can he get success.

6. Addiction

Video game is said to be addiction. Children from these games also learn to become the actual user of drugs and alcohol. Parents fail to know when their child has become a victim of intoxication.

7. Sexual Abuse

It cannot be known by children while playing video games as to when they have become victims of sexual abuse. Video games are among the most effective online disorders. Children are not always at fault. Parents are as guilty as the children. Children play video games with their friends till midnight and the parents do not know what their children are doing. They also might have played video games in their childhood, but in old day's games and today's games, there is a lot of difference. The truth is that with the advent of new technology every day, the entire format of technology has changed. Earlier, children were not connected to the online media as much as they are nowadays. The Industry of video games is very big and the most beneficial. Their founders continue to explain benefits of video games, but the reality is that such games are a threat to their lives. It is a pity that parents keep scolding children when they lie, steal, eat junk food etc but they do not prohibit them from playing violent video games. It is because of the simple reason when children are busy with their videos, they do not disturb their parents. So much so to avoid disturbance from children parents encourage them to play video games.

Video games used during the decade of the eighties were not only the medium of entertainment for children but those games also increased the skill of maintaining the balance of hands and eyes besides increasing the ability of concentration. These were all off-line games. In the decade of nineties, online games came into the market which can be played by children on their phones. Earlier games of the eighties were played by a single child at a time. New games that are coming nowadays can not only be played by many children at one given time. They can also become its partners. They can create their virtual characters also and through them, they can do everything they should not do in real life. If the problem is limited to that then there was no danger. Astonishingly but now some games are becoming a terrible threat to the children.

Children do not have this danger from any kidnapper, thief, robber or enemy. This threat to children is from social media platforms and unusual games. At first, when the children used to go out of the house to play football, cricket, kabaddi, then their parents remained worried for them. Now when the children sit in the house and play video games for hours, parents think that the children are secure inside the house. This is their biggest mistake because some of the games, played by the children in their home may lead them to commit crimes, to get the experience of practical sex and later to sexually abuse children. Some of these games may cost their life.

Blue Whale and Other Dangerous Games

The video game called Blue Whale is a suicidal game said to have been started in Russia in the year of 2013. The group that started this game is known as the Death Group, which is also called as "F57" and this game is played in almost 50 countries. This is not a common game. In this game, children are given the challenge of doing a dangerous job every day for 50 days. Children playing this game have to send actual photos or videos of their daily work showing the dare devil act of their work to the administrator of the game for having done the job as per his requirement. These challenges are not common but are dangerous as if looking at horror movies at midnight, going to a deserted place alone in the night darkness, writing something with own blood on the arms, and ultimately to committing suicide.

In this game, the curator first collects full information about children and their families and also collects secret information, if any, about them so that they are able to blackmail children. The curator gradually induces mind of children to believe that this world is not worthy of their living and as such they must leave this world as soon as possible. If children refuse to obey them, the curator threatens them about their family, threatens to publish their secret information. Such criminals make children their targets because children are ignorant and they do not have the ability to handle such like situations. Most of such children become victims of these criminals who are not mentally healthy or who are living in some tension due to any reason. Consequently, the children are not able to decide what is good for them and what is bad.

According to a report published in the year 2016 in Russian newspaper Novaya Gazeta, 80 children committed suicide due to the Blue Whale game in Russia. It is said that even in India, some children have attempted suicide. Two of them already committed.

The dangers of this game called Blue Whale can be judged by the detailed report prepared by Mr. Will Stewart on the basis of the information collected by him from the officer who investigated the death cases related to this game in Russia. This Report was published in The Daily Mail on 10th may, 2017. According to the report, the inventor of a game called Blue Whale says that children who commit suicide by playing this game are mentally ill and by killing such mental patients, he is releasing the society from these patients. The inventor of this game has taken control of the mind of many children and such children are said to love him very much. In Russia, when he was caught and put behind the bars love letters of many girls were recovered from him. The Psychologists believe that these letters might have been written by those girls who could neither get any love from their parents nor they were taken care of by them. Taking advantage of their weakness, the inventor of the game might have lured them with his love on the internet. He might have given them emotional support. The children longing for love began to obey his every command. Some other Death Groups are also working online for similar activities. The officials believe that there may be hundreds of such cases in Russia alone where girls were lured in false love affair by these criminals and later pushed them in the mouth of death. The report further explains how death groups work on the online.

The controller of this game and his companions attract the children to social media by first showing them scary and dangerous videos. Their only goal is to attract as many children as possible. Of these, then they sort out the children who can be psychologically influenced. Suppose only 20 children of 15,000 thousand children come under their influence, they first start assigning them very easy tasks. Children, who are mentally strong, take these simple things as boring and leave them. But the children who accept their advice are assigned more difficult tasks such as walking on a rooftop mound, cutting a vein of their hands, killing any animal etc. Then the children are asked to create images or videos of the works done and to send to him. At this stage, most of the children stop playing any more. But some children keep playing even further as per given directions. Such children continue obeying their orders with closed eyes and shut minds even if the tasks assigned are very scary, horrific or deadly. By reaching this stage such children feel proud of themselves only by thinking that they have performed all the brave deeds. Their importance increased in the group. These children, who are proud, now look forward to doing anything more challenging.

The investigating officer told that when the game's administrator asked some children to delete the conversation on their mobile phone, all the other children deleted the conversation as directed except one girl. The girl who did not delete informed that the children can easily be fooled in this game. She further told that like other children, she used to spend most of her time on the net. One day on social media, she saw a link and clicked on one scary picture, then on the second image and finally, she joined a group that encouraged suicide. There were thousands of such groups on social media and it was very easy to join these groups. After joining a group when she completed the simple tasks given to her, she was included in a small group of children. This group directed her to start chatting at 4.00 in the night. She was asked to chat for one night, two nights, three nights and nights after nights till she got tired and exhausted. Waking up every night at four and chatting as per their orders she got so tired and helpless she was left with no power to think about anything else. It was a terrible job. When the rest of the world was sleeping in the darkness of the night, her phone used to ring up suddenly and new videos were shown to me every minute. In these videos, children were shown jumping down from the roof of their house. Such close-ups were shown in which the bodies of the children were soaked in blood. Blood oozing out of their mouths and scattered all around their bodies. Not only this, there will be very scary music in the background mixed with the sound of the crying animals It appeared as if children were being tortured and they were sobbing and crying of pain in loud voices.

Gripped in the panic I was thinking either to commit suicide or to kill someone else.

She once posted that I want to leave this group. In response, she started getting threats from them. She was told that I am a worthless creature, and she should hate myself living such a worthless life. Rather I should get rid of such a devious life. I was forced to watch the video till I deleted all my conversations. Not to talk of children after seeing such horrible video, even adult will get scared. The girl further told that after this she was asked to watch another video of horror music on a black screen. It was shown that a girl standing on the railway track suddenly jumped on the railway line and her body was mutilated, cut into several pieces within no time. The entire surrounding was filled with her roaring cries, screams bloodshed and scattered pieces of her organs. I am a child even adults may get scared of seeing such horrible way of ending one's life. After watching such a horrible act of committing suicide heart beatings of anyone can come to halt. After watching this video I also decided to end my devious life. It is worthless because there can be no improvement in my life in this world. He told me to finish my life as there is no one who loves me or takes care of me. Even my parents also do not like me. So it would be better to end such a useless life, the administrator explained. He explained that he had chosen me to commit suicide as I was a very intelligent and a wise girl. He further said they are lucky, who are chosen to commit suicide and I am equally lucky that I have come to understand the reality of my futile life.

He ordered me to be wise enough to present an example of doing a great job of committing suicide and do not delay this work. I was nervous and hesitated to accept their last order. Seeing my hesitation he gave me a second suggestion. He said that if I am afraid of jumping from the roof or coming under the moving train then I should consume poison. I will not have any problem in my death. According to him, I set the time. But God was very pleased that I was saved from committing suicide in time.

The culprit is now in a Russian jail. When he was asked if he had motivated the children to commit suicide, he shyly accepted and said yes, I have not only motivated many children, but many children have obeyed me and committed suicide They did not commit suicide, but they gladly gave their lives because they wanted to. With great shamelessness he further told that in his opinion all the children who came to commit suicide were mentally ill. Such children were the waste of society and by encouraging them to commit suicide, I was cleaning the society with this garbage. They had no proper use for the society, nor could they do anything good for the society. Hence their death was in the interest of the society. I was working on it for the past five years and in the year 2013; I started this program by introducing F7 (On-Line). My objective was to separate the litter of society from the good class of society. The content of my social media was to create depression. This type of material first used to influence children with my thoughts. After being well-nurtured, the children were taken online in such a system, where all i wanted was available. At this stage, we start with the Blue Whale Game by giving simple tasks to children. Gradually the intimate conversation was started with the children, which makes us know how much worth these children were. After getting the required information from the children, I used to hypnotize them by talking on Skype to collect all the information relating to their life in the state of their hypnosis. Sometimes children had to be taken to a sleepy state in order to get very secret information because, in such a situation, all secret information could be obtained from them. This method was more successful than it was expected. So successful that some people started working to deceive children by imitating me and my name, and many people are still doing this work. They have created many death groups which inspire children to commit suicide.

A lot has been mentioned in this report about how this criminal created a program to kill children. He told to the Investigating Officer that he had no friends in his school. Both mother and father used to work far away from home. They took a lot of time to come back home. He often took to fight with other children in the school. He was also weak in the studies. After school, he used to play online games for hours. He further told that while living alone and playing only online games he thought himself to be his own boss. Suddenly he thought he can be the owner of the life and thoughts of other people also. Thereafter he thought of making this killer Blue Whale game. By this he could instigate many a children commit suicide. It has been observed that children who live on internet and lonely life are prone to such death traps. They first loose hope, and, then jump to boredom. This finally leads to death trap. The investigating officer also told the reporter how the children trapped in his game had been committing suicide. He used to induce them mentally ready for taking such a drastic step. It was done by shedding the fear of death from their minds. In Russia, two girls committed suicide due to a game called Blue Whale. Another girl committed suicide by jumping from the twelfth floor by logging in a group called Wake Me Up at 4.20. It is said that in this group, millions of children used to play games. The girl was told that she is fat and she will only have to eat a little salad. Within 50 days of joining the group, she committed suicide. A 16-year-old Ukrainian girl committed suicide by jumping from the tenth floor. Her friends told that she was a very shy girl. In school, they had seen signs of cutting on her arms. Prior to her death, she posted a picture of the scene taken from a high building on his social network page and wrote that "the wait is over; it is just a step away now. She wrote further "I did not know it could be so scary to jump down from such a height. But by just stepping forward one step, all will end. But this last step seems to be the most difficult step. Before jumping from the high rise building she again wrote, I'm very scared, I am very much scared. Despite this, the girl jumped down from the tenth floor and died instantly.

Criminals, first of all, provide easy works to children, then difficult, then more difficult, extremely difficult, they are asked to perform scary works and finally to do extremely terrible works to do. Thus they make them fearless and inspire them to commit suicide.

10

Other Killer Games

In the world of social media, the Blue Whale Game is not the only game that inspires children to commit suicide. There are so many other games that are dangerous for children.

HIGH SCHOOL GANGSTER ESCAPE

The Blue Whale Challenge, a task-based 'game' is not a single game that many children fell for. There are many other games available. Both on Android and iOS platforms. They are equally dangerous for young minds. There is a new game called "High School Gangster Escape" Shortly before, the Blue Whale game surfaced came into the discussion in which the children used to commit suicide in the last stage of playing the game, a new game came up in which children do not commit suicide but they are induced to commit murder of other persons. This game has been detected recently by the double murder in Greater Noida where a 16-years old boy killed his mother and sister. A day after a 16-year-old boy allegedly killed his 42-year-old mother and 11-year-old sister in a high rise society in Greater Noida, Investigators said that the boy was a compulsive gamer who might have been influenced by High School gangster Escape, a game he used to play on his mobile phone.

What is this game?

The hero of the high school gangster game gives flying kiss to the girls, steals the food from the Tiffin of other students, steals Examination papers, throws paper balls on the back of the teacher and works like teasing the other students. If someone tries to stop him, the hero even murders. It is being speculated that this game has had a bad effect on the mind of the boy who killed his mother and sister in Greater Noida.

If you read about the features of this game, which suggest it is about committing crimes and escaping. There are chances that the children, addicted to this game may commit more such like crimes, under the influence of the game.

City High School Revenge Game

This game is similar to High School gangster game. In this game, children also carry out violence in the school. The story and plot is also similar to Gangster Game. The game provides tricks to children how to escape from the security guard and police after committing a crime.

High School Evil Teacher

This game relates to the torture of students by a bad teacher. There is a bad teacher inside the school who harasses students and enjoys the acute corporal punishment. Some children also support the teacher and torture many innocent children.

High School Gangster Robbery

In this game children studying in High School have to become a gangster. After becoming Gangster, a Robbery Plan is chalked out. After the robbery, they plan an escape route as to how to dodge the people and the city police. There is everything in this game violence, theft, robbery, guns, and, there are criminals all over the city.

Pokémon-Go

This is a video game in which children have to purchase various types of attractive animals called Pokémon. This is a type of business game that is online but played in real life too. While playing the game, children feel like Pokémon is going to the real places using their phone's GPS and camera. Children start searching for those places looking for Pokémon. In this search, children keep concentrating on their phones unaware of their surroundings. They do not have the attention of the road nor do they look at the traffic unmindful of onward coming traffic on road they keep on walking looking at the Pokémon in their mobile in hand. The children playing this game often become victims of the road accidents. The intoxication of this game is so dominant on the children that they sometimes fall into the river, streams of the pond. Many a times they jump down from high rise buildings.

Children looking for their pokémon become victims of accidents. It will not be out of place to say that many children throughout the world have already lost their lives playing this game.

1. During the game, children may also meet some unknown people whom they do not even recognize. One of its games is called Raids in which many people play this game together. But children do not recognize all those people. Some of them may be offenders, who can harm them.
2. Children playing this game do not know where they are going to find Pokémon. According to the available facts, children can also reach a place that is not safe for them.
3. Waste of money: In this game, children have to pay some money; only then the game goes ahead. The real money is paid in this purchase. Addicted to the game children may not know that they have spent a lot of money to play this game.
4. Fear of personal information: In this game, children are asked for personal information. Their name, date of birth, e-mail address. This information is sought from the children to open their social media accounts. It can well be misused.

This game has been created by the makers of Google Maps. So, in this game, Smartphone cameras have been arranged to find real locations with the help of Google Map. Every child has a Smartphone in hand. Spirit of the game is also in all children. Its proper use is helpful, but wrong use can lead to the death of children.

Other Games of Pokémon

In this game, the players have to catch different kinds of small creatures with the help of objects like circular guides which are called pokey-balls. The creatures to be caught are also of different kinds. Their speed, gait, temperaments, and activeness also differ from each other. The player who catches the maximum number of creatures is declared Pokey-master and winner of the game.

Pokémon Gyms

The main part of this game is the tall buildings that can be anywhere in the world. Players compete with each other to search them with the help of Google maps. In this search, they get deeply lost, that they forget about their position and become victims of the accident.

Pokémon Raids

This is a type of war that many players play together. In this game, everyone has to get points after defeating their red-boss rival in the war. Children need a pass to participate in this war. Every player can get only one pass in a day. If more passes are required, then they have to buy by paying real money. Needless to say, the game is never completed with the help of one pass and the children have to buy more and more unwanted passes.

On the one hand, there is a loss of money and on the other hand, children come in contact with strangers who may turn evils later. There is every likelihood they are doing business. Not charity.

In August 2017, a program in NDTV was shown on TV about some other video games that could lead to the death of children like:

Vampire Biting

The name of the game proves itself to be a game of behaving like vampire full of bloodshed. In this game, players have to behave like a vampire in their real life and have to bite the flesh of the people around them by cutting with their teeth. When children become vampires and bite others, their blood flows. This blood may go into the mouth of player also. The blood of other people gets directly connected to the mouth of the player. If the person who is beaten by the player is suffering from an infection with diseases like HIV, Hepatitis etc, the player can also be a victim of these diseases. This was told during TV show on NDTV in August 2017.

Snorting Challenge

Everyone can understand by the very name of this game that it relates to the ability to sniff. But the surprise is that it not snorting of some smells any fragrance or deodorant. In this game, children challenge each other to snort certain things through their nose and bring them out through their mouth. One cannot think about the items which children use in this game. It can be anything like balloons, strings, or any other item. One can easily understand such thing may be a cause of death for any child.

When the name of Challenge has emerged, parents may know that there are thousands of games by the name of Challenge easily available on YouTube where different challenges are offered to children in the form of games. In these games, children are asked to complete different types of hazardous tasks which can be a danger to their life. A few games are described below:–

Game of 72

The game of 72 is a challenge among teenagers to vanish for 72 hours. Essentially children are daring each other to "go dark" for 72 hours. To kids going dark for 72 hours means to make themselves go.

In this game, children are asked to run away from home for 72 hours. Children go somewhere without informing their parents about 72 hours or so. When the children do not come home the parents get worried. They start searching for their children. After having done an exhaustive search when parents fail to find the whereabouts of children they report the matter of kidnapping with local police. In the meantime, the friends of the missing child, who are involved in the game, try to search him through this game. The player who is able to search for the missing child is declared the winner.

In this game, children may choose a place to hide which can be dangerous for their life. Moreover in their absence parents under shock may fall seriously ill and sometimes due to serious shock they may die also.

The Car Surfing Challenge

In this game, children are asked to perform dangerous acts on the moving car. Lying on the moving car's bonnet or standing on a bumper they are asked to perform different acts. While performing acts on moving cars if the balance of their body is disturbed, the death of children is certain.

Chocking Game:

This is a very funny and gimmick game in which the players press each other's throats. The player who tolerates the throat pressure for a maximum time becomes the winner. The child who presses the throat of other child uses full power to press his throat so that he will give up soon. On the other hand, the child who is pressed in the throat tries to feel the pressure of stress on his neck more than his strength. In any case, he does not want to lose. The child who thrives on his throat increases his pressure. After a limit of bearing the heavy pressure on the throat child may die.

God knows there are how many such games that are playing with the life of children. Perhaps the parents are not aware of where such videos come from.

The Origin of the Dangerous Videos

The internet is much broader than what we think. There are many things that are hidden from most people. Nor can everyone find them all. Then which can be such a site where the children reach and get stuck in the dangerous games? The common people recognize only the Facebook, Google etc. Apart from these trusted sites, there is a lot on the Internet.

There is a small link in the corner of the Internet known as Dark Net or Deep Web. These sites are not easily visible but remain hidden on the internet. To access these sites, a special type of software is used which is called TOR. With the help of this software, game operators interact with children for which they use illegal methods and do not get caught by anyone. Let's try to understand them.

What is Dark Web?

Dark Web is the name of a network that contains a collection of many Web sites whose script is encrypted. This cannot be opened by a common search engine or traditional web browser. Almost all the sites hide their identity with the help of software called TOR. With the help of TOR, they not only hide their identity and misdeeds but also conceal those who use it and keep their activities hidden. With the help of TOR software, people can dodge their living place also. They can show the place of their residence in another country. This hides their identity in a sensual way. It is possible through VPN i.e. virtual private network. People providing VPN services keep secret any conversation done by people on their computers, phones or tablets. They maintain this secrecy by changing the people's actual IP address by providing a fictitious IP Address. Like an onion, they put layers one upon another in many layers on the contents of users to hide their identity. Anybody can use the dark website but it is difficult to find out who is managing to run this website. With a little mistake by the user, his all information including secret information can be disclosed and made known to culprits.

Going to Dark Web or Dark Net is technically no difficult task. Just install TOR and use it. You need to download the TOR browser bundle by visiting www.torproject.org where all the necessary tools are available. After running downloaded file, you can choose what you want to see. After making the choice, clicking on the folder starts using TOR. After going to the dark web, all those sites are available whatever you want, such as drugs, sex, guns and even more.

The Deep Web is even More Misleading

If you are looking at the dark web or the darknet sites, they all look like similar sites. They are alike but there is a little difference between them. The pages of Deep Web cannot be seen on any search engine. In Deep Web, not only the dark web is included, but it also keeps the personal information of the people who use Deep Web. The biggest thing is that those who work on Deep Web continue to see their work, but if others want to see they need to have a password to see it on search engine otherwise it will not appear on any search engine.

The purpose of describing these sites here is just to apprise parents about existence of such sites. There are many more such sites/material available on the internet. They can be very dangerous for children. Not in any one or two cases but nowadays most children are facing sexual abuse, violence, drugs, kidnapping threats on the internet including children of all ages. Children cannot be distinguished according to age. It will be better to see how children can overcome these dangers. It is also a big question whether all children are able to keep themselves safe or not. Children will be safe only when the parents themselves will understand the safe use of technology. So it is absolutely essential that the parents understand at least that much technology with the help of which their children can be protected.

Parents must first ensure that their children use technology as minimum as possible. All efforts should be made to give more importance to the real world than the digital world. This will help in making children aware of the importance of real life. They will also be able to know about their own importance and their own power. This way, children will be motivated simply not to waste their precious time using technology and playing different types of games but to use it only for their required essential tasks.

Many parents do not know anything about technology. Those, whose children use technology should at least get some information about it so that they can know what their children are doing on their Smartphone.

In the Field of Technology, Children are Ahead of Their Parents

Some parents do not even know how the computer or laptop functions, what are Apps and what is WiFi meant for. They even do not know what YouTube is. Such parents should learn something about technology and get some basic information so that they can monitor the online activities of their children.

When a child has to face danger, then he goes running in the protected shelter of his parents. He knows that only his parents can save him from every danger. Parents will be able to help children only if they themselves are capable of facing the danger. If parents are ignorant then how will they save their children from dangers? The parents who do not have much knowledge of the Internet, their children keep on using on-line arbitrariness without any control. Nowadays, children are in danger everywhere, whether they are online or offline. The matter of friends or relatives is different; children are most dependent on their parents.

If the children are to be protected from any danger, then parents will have to share their problems. They must recognize their wishes. Not only will they have to fulfill the duty as parents but also that of friends. If the parents do not protect their children, then no other person can do this work. Therefore, the parent will have to obtain the necessary information of the Internet. Nowadays children cannot be left alone with Facebook, What's App, YouTube or My Space. The parents will have to take their command in their own hands

Anyway, the children have now moved forward from their parents. Social networking on Facebook is now an old case for them. They adopt a new technique every day, which parents do not even know. But there is no need for parents to panic about this problem and neither do they need to acquire knowledge of all kinds of new techniques. They will have to pay attention to some of the main techniques, especially on the techniques that can be a cause of danger to children. Looking at the habits of children, they have to take care of some basic things only.

Some websites and apps are very popular among children. Children keep using them all the time. Now kids do not stick to Facebook only. They now have other tools such as Instagram, Snapchat, What's App, and Twitter, which they stick on for the day. So it is necessary to know what the children do on these sites and whether there can be any threat to them. Some websites and apps are being mentioned below, which are more liked by children. Parents should know about these and other such sites.

Texting Apps

Message (Giving or Receiving)

There are many more apps available today, on which children can send and receive their messages for free. Not only messages, children can also exchange photos, videos and attachment links also. When a facility is available for free of cost, children may use it to their maximum extent. If children are using this technology for their study or to enhance their knowledge it is the best use, otherwise, it can be harmful.

Caution:

Parents should know that some apps are suitable only for older children because they contain some material in GIF (Graphic Interchange Format) and Emojis for adults only, such as drug abuse or sexual activity and criminal activity. Being free and unlimited children like to use them more and more. This facility is available to all, so in the case of texting, children may come into contact with many unknown people. Children because of their tender age are not able to know which contact of unknown people is good or bad. People with the criminal background too can get access and develop contacts with children for taking their undue and illegitimate benefit. Children are tempted through ads on some apps too. They are attracted to buy inappropriate or prohibited items through these ads. The drug content or sexual content cannot be easily found in the open market but it can be bought online without any difficulty.

Whats App

The Whats App Company has prohibited its use by the children under the age of 13 years. It has a simple meaning that small children should not use it. The special reason for this is that after opening the account on Whats App, the children come in contact with all those available in their address book who are using Whats App. Through the Whats App, all people can send unlimited messages, text, video, audio, photos to single or multiple people without limits. Though the child can use it within their group but still parents should have to be careful because:–

- It does not require any password, as such criminal minded people, through any of the members of the group can join the group. It becomes easy for criminals to make contact with children once they have joined the group. As a member of the group then they can send inappropriate and dangerous messages to children.

- The children may receive any kind of inappropriate message, video or photo on the Whats App, which can contaminate their thinking and their ideas. Facebook, YouTube and some other networks do not permit posting of inappropriate or sexual photos, videos, audio, but there is no such restriction on Whats App. However it is prohibited by law Sec. 67 of the I.T. Act 2008 in India.

The absence of passwords or posting photos or videos would not be so alarming, but the main danger is from criminal minded people. These people, by using a special technique called grooming, can collect personal information and the identity of children. Thereafter they select children who can be made the victim of their crimes. After getting the necessary information, these people contact the children selected through Facebook or any other safe network. After contacting children they befriend them, intensity their relationship and gradually win over their trust. Once they win the trust, the culprits start sending private messages. These private messages gradually become inappropriate and offensive. In this way, Whats Apps is a boon for the offenders. Through this medium any type of information can be exchanged without any restriction and free of cost in an unlimited manner.

Caution
WhatsApp

- Children can come into contact with strangers, few of which can be offenders.
- Unknown people can see children's profile.
- Some messages may also be related to crime or scandals.
- Drugs and sexual information can be sent.

Camera and Video

Nowadays there is no Smartphone without a camera and video facility. The benefit of this facility is more because it gives people the opportunity to work creatively. Elders may use this facility in creative use, but children after all are children. They do whatever they like to. It is true that whats app is a very popular medium but in addition to this, there are many other mediums available which are frequently used by children in the way they like without the knowledge of their parents. Many times parents are in dark about the online activities of their children on following systems:–

Instagram
Flicker
Google photos
Amazon Photos
Snap fish
Imgur
500px (500px)
Drop box

The list can be very long and it will be difficult for everyone to understand. Sharing photo, video, a text is common practice, people even share the smallest events relating to their home or connected with the children. Children are more skilled in this art. Sharing with friends and family members is usual. So far so good. A few people know the dangers associated with it, especially those who have less knowledge of the dangers of sharing photos. In order to protect the children, the parent will have to pay attention to some essential points like:–

Sharing Photos

After having shared a photo by a person on any digital platform, he loses his control over the shared photograph. Anyone can copy, tag, or save this photo. It can also be not known who is doing so. Some terms and conditions are written on almost every site of social media but nobody cares to read them. One of these conditions is written in very small letters or in hidden form so that this condition cannot be easily read. The condition is,

> *"You abandon ownership, copyright, and consent to what you have shared on the platform of our social media."*

Meaning thereby they can use the content you shared on their platform for whatsoever purpose without your permission.

Identity is Disclosed

According to the conditions, the sender of photo loses the control of the photo shared by him. A fewer people know that along with the shared photo their personal information can also be collected by unscrupulous people, which can be misused. Even if the collected information is not used by them immediately but it can always be used after a considerable amount of time. There is every likelyhood.

Data Collection

Nowadays, data collection is a big business. People keep creating thousands of data points per day, especially about the children. Where do children go, to whom they talk with, what do they talk about, what do they read, what they write, what do they buy, what do they say, what do they see, when they go to school, how do they go, when do they come back, when do they sleep when they wake up. There is no such activity in life that the data collector is not looking at. The information shared on any site immediately goes to a lot of people, including private individuals, marketers, financial institutions, government offices, and criminals. If the information related to children reaches to strangers it can be harmful to them. The parents can also be harassed if their information is collected by strange and unknown people.

The importance of personal information may not have any significance in the eyes of the people, but they do not perhaps know that collecting personal information of people is a very big business nowadays. The personal information is sold now at very high prices. Buyers make profiles of people with the help of their personal information. There is no control over how many people make how many such profiles. According to news, an attempt was made to sell the infant related material to a pregnant woman, and the fact that the woman did not give the information about being pregnant to any of her relatives or acquaintances. This means that her personal information was collected from social media without the permission of the woman and it was also used. Similarly, any data obtained from any site can be collected and be sold. The buyer is free to use any data purchased by him because after sharing the data the person who shared it loses his control of the shared data. Children thus easily become victims of criminals because they keep on sharing even sensitive private data every now and then.

Data Theft

Collecting and using someone's personal information against rules for financial benefits is called data theft. This can be theft of somebody's social security, it can also be used to open an account in the bank or hack the bank account. Data theft of personal information of anyone can be dangerous. There are several methods to steal the data of anyone that is available on the net. Nowadays personal information of every person is available in the electronic system in more than required quantity. This can be a reason that criminal activities are increasing day by day particularly in the case of children. Nowadays the information which is collected in the school forms is not only personal but sensitive also. Parents are unable to know how this information given to schools is collected by criminals and then used for crime. The most horrific threat to children is their abduction. There can be the online digital kidnapping of children.

Digital Kidnapping

Children's records are available at the site of the school, on the site of relatives; the parents continue sharing the information related to the children. The important and sensitive information is available in the accounts of children also. These are all such sites where from criminals collect the required information related to the children. The stolen information or photographs so collected is then sold at high prices to producer companies or advertising companies. After this, the stolen information or photographs related to the children is used by the buyers for their financial benefits. Parents or children themselves do not know who is using their photos and how they are doing it. The persons who have stolen the photos or the persons who have purchased the stolen photos would post these stolen photographs on different websites pretending them to be photographs of their own children. They pretend as if they are the real parents of these children. Thus children are digitally kidnapped. One day Mr. Goyal to spend some time was searching on his Smartphone in his free time. Suddenly he was shocked to see a photograph of her daughter Pari on one peculiar site. He was surprised as to who had posted the photo of his daughter Pari on an unknown site and for what purpose? For more information, he examined the profile of Pari and found that some person of the name of Jackson was claiming Pari to be his daughter. He was proposing to sell her photograph for advertisement. He was even prepared to sell her photo for sexual advertisement if given more money. Mr. Goyal was so worried about her daughter that he lost his sleep. He never knew as to who was using photos of her daughter and for what purpose. What will he do next?

Next with the help of stolen photographs of children their fake accounts with fake names and fake identity are opened. Thereafter the comments of people are invited to such fake profiles of children. God knows what else they do with stolen photos. Some offenders even make their fake families and invite offers from people to adopt these children. Children sometimes out of excitement can also post such material which can be very dangerous for them.

Every post made on the internet becomes a matter of record. This contains all the information that is shared on the Internet. Only a few people will know that unknown people can see their every activity carried out on the internet, and they can also use it. In digital language, it is called Footprint. Word meaning of footprint is signs of the foot. It means other people can identify by the signs of the activities done on the internet about the person using the internet. His personal information is thus collected through his on-line activities.

What is Foot Print?

A digital footprint is a trail of data you create while using the internet. It includes the websites you visit, emails you send, and information you submit to online services. The activities that are done by children on Internet leave behind certain signs which are called Footprints. These footprints can be created by the use of e-mail, registration, attachment, uploading video or exchange of information of any kind or other types of information leaving such marks on the internet. All such activities leave behind personal information of children on the internet.

Any activity done by children on the internet leaves behind some trail of footprints. With the help of these footprints unknown people may collect important information related to them. Some information is given by the children themselves, it is called Active Data like Facebook, Twitter, Blog Post, Social Media Network, Uploading Video, Photo, Email, Phone Call and Chat etc. Apart from this, some information relating to children is posted by other people also using the internet. Sometimes children may also use information relating to them. Every type of information posted on any type of media becomes a permanent record. Once this record is posted in the public, it goes out of the control of its user. Unknown people can also use such information available on the media for whatever purpose they wish and they cannot be stopped by the owner of the information.

In simple words whatever activity is done on the internet, its information gets recorded automatically. This recorded information can be used by anyone without the permission of the actual user. A digital footprint is permanent information that cannot be erased or deleted. The information in digital footprints may include your personal identity, who you are, where do you live, what do you do, what is your address, and what is your phone number etc If you have to use the Internet then you have to face it and also have to defend yourself. For the safety of the children, parents should have the following information:–

1. What is Digital Footprint?

All of the work that we do on the Internet, like commenting on social media, talking on Skype, using apps, or emailing it all gets recorded online and potentially in the reach of others Or can be collected by others in their database.

2. How Foot Prints are Created?

There are as many ways to leave a footprint as there are many ways to use the internet. Not all methods can be mentioned, but some necessary methods are described below:

3. Online Shopping and Website

When searching on a website or doing online shopping, the vendor and similar companies drop out some cookies on the system of the searcher, with the help of which they keep tracking every activity of internet users.

4. Social Media

Every activity that is done on the social media also gets recorded. Private setting is also not safe. Some social sites continue to tell new policies or settings of privacy, with the help of which they will be able to access all the information related to their use.

5. Mobile Phones, Tablets or Laptops

People keep searching for many things on different websites. Which site have you visited, what did you do there, a complete list of your all activities gets prepared which can be used by the owners of the concerned Website. They may not use your information to harm you but they can collect your personal information in their system.

OTHER BOOKS YOU MAY LIKE

- A Christmas Carol by Charles Dickens, ISBN: 9788193545874
- A Midsummer Night's Dream by William Shakespeare, ISBN: 9789380914510
- A Tear and a Smile by Kahlil Gibran, ISBN: 9788180320477
- Apni Chhamta Pehchaniye (Hindi) by NK Sondhi, ISBN: 9788193545843
- As a Man Thinketh by James Allen, ISBN: 9788180320262
- As You Like It by William Shakespeare, ISBN: 9789380914459
- Believe in Yourself by Joseph Murphy, ISBN: 9789388118385
- Be What You Wish by Neville Goddard, ISBN: 9789387669550
- Because Every Raindrop is a Hope by Sankalp Kohli, ISBN: 9789380914435
- Children's Classic Rhymes by Various Authors, ISBN: 9788193545805
- Children's Classic Stories by Aniesha Brahma, ISBN: 9788193545812
- Children's Objective Quiz by Dr. Ruth Premi, ISBN: 9788180320781
- Civilization and Its Discontents by Sigmund Freud, ISBN: 9789387669499
- Favourite Tales from the Arabian Nights by Sir Richard F. Burton, ISBN: 9789380914077
- Gita According to Gandhi by Mahatma Gandhi, ISBN: 9788180320040
- Gravity by George Gamow, ISBN: 9789388118484
- Great German Short Stories by Various Authors, ISBN: 9789380914053
- Great Speeches of Abraham Lincoln by Abraham Lincoln, ISBN: 9789380914336
- Hamlet by William Shakespeare, ISBN: 9789380914466
- How to Attract Money by Joseph Murphy, ISBN: 9789388118408
- How to Develop Self-Confidence & Impr. Pub. Speaking by Carnegie, ISBN: 9789387669000
- How to Enjoy Your Life and Your Job by Dale Carnegie, ISBN: 9789387669017
- How to Stop Worrying and Start Living by Dale Carnegie, ISBN: 9789380914817
- Illust. Biography of William Shakespeare by Manju Gupta, ISBN: 9788180320941
- Julius Caesar by William Shakespeare, ISBN: 9789380914374
- Love Happens only Once by Rochak Bhatnagar, ISBN: 9789380914183
- Macbeth by William Shakespeare, ISBN: 9789380914343
- Madhubala by Manju Gupta, ISBN: 9789380914961
- Mansarover 2 (Hindi) by Premchand, ISBN: 9789380914985
- Mat Cheeno Bachpan (Hindi) by NK Sondhi, ISBN: 9789387669895

Develop your reading habit | **Gift books to your friends**

OTHER BOOKS YOU MAY LIKE

- Mein Kampf (My Struggle) by Adolf Hitler, ISBN: 9789380914855
- Metamorphosis by Franz Kafka, ISBN: 9788180320057
- Mother by Maxim Gorky, ISBN: 9788180320330
- My Experiments with Truth by Mahatma Gandhi, ISBN: 9789387669291
- My Inventions: The Autobiography of Nikola Tesla by Tesla, ISBN: 9789388118132
- My Life : Albert Einstein by GP Editors, ISBN: 9789388118941
- My Life : Dilip Kumar by GP Editors, ISBN: 9789388118934
- One Life, One Love by Rochak Bhatnagar, ISBN: 9789380914350
- Othello by William Shakespeare, ISBN: 9789380914404
- Our Imperfectly Perfect Love by Rochak Bhatnagar, ISBN: 9789380914824
- Pride and Prejudice by Jane Austen, ISBN: 9789380914428
- Quiz For All by Dr. Ruth Premi, ISBN: 9788180320897
- Romeo and Juliet by William Shakespeare, ISBN: 9789380914329
- Save Your Child by NK Sondhi, ISBN: 9789388118361
- Selected Short Stories of James Joyce by James Joyce, ISBN: 9788180320392
- Selected Stories of Rabindranath Tagore by Tagore, ISBN: 9789380914770
- Sense and Sensibility by Jane Austen, ISBN: 9789380914589
- Tales from Shakespeare by Charles & Mary Lamb, ISBN: 9789380914367
- The Alchemy of Happiness by Al-Ghazzali, ISBN: 9789387669505
- The Art of Public Speaking by Dale Carnegie, ISBN: 9788180320422
- The Art of War by Sun Tzu, ISBN: 9789380914893
- The Autobiography of a Yogi by Paramahansa Yogananda, ISBN: 9789380914602
- The Autobiography of Benjamin Franklin by Benjamin, ISBN: 9788190276689
- The Bhagavad Gita by Sir Edwin Arnold, ISBN: 9789380914275
- The Canterville Ghost by Oscar Wilde, ISBN: 9789380914527
- The Dynamic Laws of Prosperity by Catherine Ponder, ISBN: 9789388118156
- The Game of Life and How to Play It by Florence S. Shinn, ISBN: 9789387669390
- The Girl I Last Loved by Smita Kaushik, ISBN: 9789380914244
- The Great Gatsby by F. Scott Fitzgerald, ISBN: 9789380914473
- The Greatest Short Stories of Leo Tolstoy by Leo Tolstoy, ISBN: 9788180320002

Develop your reading habit | **Gift books to your friends**

OTHER BOOKS YOU MAY LIKE

- The Imitation of Christ by Thomas À Kempis, ISBN: 9789388118057
- The Invisible Man by H.G. Wells, ISBN: 9788193545850
- The Jungle Book by Rudyard Kipling, ISBN: 9788193545867
- The Little Prince by Antoine De Saint-Exupéry, ISBN: 9788180320590
- The Magic of Believing by Claudie Bristol, ISBN: 9789388118149
- The Magic of Faith by Joseph Murphy, ISBN: 9789388118743
- The Merchant of Venice by William Shakespeare, ISBN: 9789380914497
- The Miracles of Your Mind by Joseph Murphy, ISBN: 9788180320743
- The Origin of Species by Charles Darwin, ISBN: 9788180320453
- The Power of Awareness by Neville Goddard, ISBN: 9789387669406
- The Power of Concentration by Theron Q. Dumont, ISBN: 9789388118064
- The Power of Positive Thinking by Norman Vincent Peale, ISBN: 9789388118569
- The Prince by Niccolò Machiavelli, ISBN: 9789387669024
- The Prophet by Kahlil Gibran, ISBN: 9789380914022
- The Psychopathology of Everyday Life by Sigmund Freud, ISBN: 9789388118071
- The Quick and Easy Way to Effec. Speaking by Dale Carnegie, ISBN: 9789387669031
- The Seven Laws of Teaching by John Milton Gregory, ISBN: 9789387669413
- The Story of My Life by Helen Keller, ISBN: 9789380914541
- The Tempest by William Shakespeare, ISBN: 9789380914657
- The Time Machine by HG Wells, ISBN: 9789387669048
- The Upanishads by Swami Paramananda, ISBN: 9789388118750
- The Wit and Wisdom of Gandhi by Mahatma Gandhi, ISBN: 9789380914039
- Think and Grow Rich by Napoleon Hill, ISBN: 9788180320255
- Three Men in a Boat by Jerome K. Jerome, ISBN: 9789380914442
- Treasure Island by Robert Louis Stevenson, ISBN: 9788193545881
- Twelfth Night by William Shakespeare, ISBN: 9789380914503
- Up From Slavery by Booker T. Washington, ISBN: 9789380914565
- Wake Up and Live by Dorothea Brande, ISBN: 9789387669574
- Walden and Civil Disobedience by Henry David Thoreau, ISBN: 9788180320507

Develop your reading habit | **Gift books to your friends**

www.ingramcontent.com/pod-product-compliance
Lightning Source LLC
Chambersburg PA
CBHW031258110426
42743CB00040B/731